CHABOT COLLEGE - HAYWARD
3 555 000
W9-CUB-200

where the pavement ends

American Indian Literature and Critical Studies Series
Gerald Vizenor and Louis Owens, General Editors

where the pavement ends
FIVE NATIVE AMERICAN PLAYS

William S. Yellow Robe, Jr.

UNIVERSITY OF OKLAHOMA PRESS : NORMAN

CHABOT COLLEGE LIBRARY

PS
3575
.E46
W48
2000

This is a work of fiction. Names, characters, places, and incidents are either the product of the author's imagination or are used fictitiously, and any resemblance to actual events, locales, or persons, living or dead, is entirely coincidental.

Library of Congress Cataloging-in-Publication Data

Yellow Robe, William S., 1960–
Where the pavement ends : five Native American plays / William S. Yellow Robe, Jr.
p. cm. — (American Indian literature and critical studies series; v. 37)
Contents: The star quilter — The body guards — Rez politics — The countil — Sneaky.
ISBN 0-8061-3265-5 (alk. paper)
1. Indians of North America—Drama. 2. Indian reservations—Drama. 3. Montana—Drama. I. Title. II. Series.
PS3575.E46 W48 2000
812′.6—dc21 00-023468

Where the Pavement Ends: Five Native American Plays is Volume 37 in the American Indian Literature and Critical Studies Series.

The paper in this book meets the guidelines for permanence and durability of the Committee on Production Guidelines for Book Longevity of the Council on Library Resources, Inc. ∞

Copyright © 2000 by the University of Oklahoma Press, Norman, Publishing Division of the University. Performance and translation rights are retained by William S. Yellow Robe, Jr. All rights reserved. Manufactured in the U.S.A.

1 2 3 4 5 6 7 8 9 10

CONTENTS

PREFACE

I have struggled with writing this, finding it difficult to say what I have to say to the people who made my writing a possibility, a reality that still contributes to my constant dreams. Thank you. I want you, the reader, to know that I will eventually get to a long list of people to thank in this preface. Some of these folks you know, others you have never heard of before, but that is all right, because I am sure they have never heard of you either.

At two different times in my mid-twenties, I remember my mother and father's telling me the same thing. My father, William Stanley Yellowrobe, Sr., said it to me first at the kitchen table as we shared a smoke and drank coffee. My mother, Mina Rose Forest-Yellowrobe, said it while sitting at the same kitchen table one night, playing a round of solitaire as I watched television.

They both asked me if I was serious about the kind of writing I was doing. I had written my first play when I was in sixth grade, under the patient and understanding Dorothy Grow, one of the kindest teachers I had at Wolf Point South Side Public School. Following that I had leapt into theater productions in junior high school and high school whenever I had the chance.

It was amazing that when I said yes, I was serious, both my parents said the same thing to me in slightly different words. What they said gave me the courage and strength to pursue my life in theater. "You'd better leave, then. Because there isn't anything for you here [on the rez]." They were right. There were no professional theater companies, very few community theater productions, just the high-school drama productions. There was nothing to support me as a playwright, actor, or director. Being young and still not sensing what they were telling me, I just shrugged and said okay. I did leave, with my first wife, Diane Louise Ruth Lamar, at my side, but I managed to return home to the Fort Peck Indian Reservation, in the small township of Wolf Point, Montana, when I got the chance.

I was honored that Diane, my wife, chose to share her life with me. It was not easy, but when you go from living as one person to living as two in order to become one, it is never easy. We were married in Wolf Point by the justice of the peace, then Diane traveled with me across the country, from one theater to the next. She was my friend, lover, confidant, and, most important, a part of my heart.

Four years after my parents left this world, Diane joined them in the journey of life. She had been diagnosed with breast cancer in 1988, one year after we were married. She wanted to divorce me after she told me, because she did not want me to be weighed down with the costs of her medical treatment. I refused, and she ended her fight in May of 1996.

During 1993–96, while I took care of Diane, I had withdrawn from playwriting to the point of its being nonexistent for me. I had been teaching at the Institute of American Indian Arts, in Santa Fe, New Mexico, but seventeen other Native faculty members and I were fired in 1996. While I was there I helped mentor young new playwrights. A fellow faculty member, Jon Davis, said to me one day, "Gee, Bill, when are you going to start doing you own work?" I did.

After my struggle to keep a small theater company, Wakiknabe, in operation, and while I was trying to find a place to live, my life finally took a strange turn for the better. Late at night on February 14, 1998, I was holding auditions for a Wakiknabe Theater Company production of Samuel Beckett's *Waiting for Godot*. I had been homeless for six weeks, with no money, and the auditions were going badly. I took a cigarette break and walked outside the small theater in the humanities building at the University of New Mexico campus in Albuquerque.

"Damn," I thought to myself. "Is this really worth it?" Fog covered the campus with a fine mist. I was not pleased with what I was seeing in the auditions, for which only four people had turned out. I was ready to call it quits when I noticed a form coming out of the fog. It was a woman who had been taking my class at the university, whom I first met back in 1996 when the other Native faculty and I were fired. She was a reporter back then and was now a student—not a teenage student, but a very bright, intelligent, beautiful grown woman.

As she walked closer to me, I was not sure whether I was having a dream or had had too much coffee and was seeing things. To my surprise, she invited me to a dance that night at one of the local Bill W. clubs. And so Lori E. Davis made a positive change in my life. She made it possible for me to continue writing while maintaining and supporting Native theater artists, including myself. Her patience, love, and understanding gave me a new surge of life that helped me to be better than I was before. I have never looked back, except to remember.

The plays were all written at different parts of my life. Some of the characters are a part of me, at one time of my life. The hardest play to write was *The Star Quilter*. I remember how much effort my mother, Mina Rose Forest-Yellowrobe, put into creating her star quilts, and it was intimidating to write a play about the art form. It also meant revisiting my experience of growing up on the reservation in northeastern Montana. It surprises me to meet people from Montana, outside the state, and see their lack of knowledge of Montana's Native nations. I still get a kick out of it today. I think Mona Grey sums up the whole experience in her last monologue.

The other plays are based on a gift my father gave to me: humor. I was always amazed by his one-liners and his unique perspective on life. I still admire Stanley Yellowrobe. He taught me to look at humanity from different points of view. He taught me how to live, love, and keep moving in life.

The Body Guards is based on a short story. It was my first play set in a specific period of time on the reservation. I have come to enjoy the simplicity of the story. After having the chance to play both Benny and Skin in two different productions, I have an even better feel for the two characters and their world.

Rez Politics is based on a short story I wrote that is part of a collection of short stories, *Things I Meant to Tell You Later*.

The story is a response to the question of who is Indian and who is not. The play's point is that being of mixed blood does not necessarily mean being Indian and white but can also mean being black and white or Asian and Indian. The Native nations of this country share blood ties with all the colors of the world.

I began writing *The Council* after a lunch meeting with the late John Kaufman. John was in Seattle participating in a reading of my full-length play, *A Stray Dog*, for the Seattle Group Theatre's Multi-Cultural Playwrights' Festival. He had been aware of my work for a year and wanted to meet me. He discussed the idea of commissioning the new play through his theater, Honolulu Theatre for Youth, and also possibly through the Seattle Children's Theatre. John was a brilliant Native theater artist. His leaving this world was a loss to many of us. What makes the play, *The Council*, exciting to me is its reaching into children's theater. I was intimidated by the possibilities before I began to write, because making this play for children meant that it really had to be good. It took me several years to get it right. I owe a thank-you to Linda Hartzell for being so patient with me. Thank you, both John Kaufman and Linda Hartzell.

Sneaky in its first draft was fourteen pages long and had only three scenes. It had a prologue that was later removed. I am very pleased with this draft. I had a chance to work with some very talented actors from the Wakiknabe Theatre Company, which made the rewriting process the most enjoyable I had had in a long time. *Sneaky* was a difficult play to write, because all three brothers represent a life that I once lived. The original title of the play was *Grandma, Why?* It was a question of why we, as people, do the things we do.

If I have one regret in writing all these plays—I think I have written a total of thirty plays to date—it is that my parents, Stanley and Mina Yellowrobe, never had a chance to see them. I wish they could have seen the productions in Seattle, New York, San Francisco, Minneapolis, and Albuquerque. I hope I have honored them in some way. It was their influence as giving and loving parents that made it possible for me to write. My mother and father did not complete high school, but they had a valuable gift they shared with me. They loved to read. As, sometimes, you do not need a church in order to pray, you do not need a classroom or an institute in order to read and learn.

Here is the list of people I want to thank. I hope I do not offend anyone whose name does not appear. Though I might not thank everyone in this book, I hope there might be another book in the future. If I list a name of someone who is no longer in this world, I ask for your forgiveness, but these people helped to make this book possible.

Among my family and friends, I would like to thank Fish/George, Carol, Mary, Josephine, Alice, Helen, Alvin, Karen, and Keith; Aunty Carol, Al John, Aunty Wilma, Grandma Alphina, Sister Caroline, Phyllis, and Joey Yellowrobe; Aunty Delila, Uncle Ed, Cousin Pat, Loren, Edna, Patty C., and a whole lot of other folks and families back in Wolf Point, Frazer, Oswego, Poplar, Brockton, and Fort Kipp, Montana.

In the academic world, I would like to thank Bill Kershner, Rolland Meinholtz, Jerry Crawford, Roger Buffalohead, Pat Smith, Ed Wapp, Steve LeBeouff, Roberta Uno, Ellsworth LeBeau, Greg Hirst, Jon Davis, John Barnes, David Krasner, Louis Owens, Jim Colbert, Arthur Sze, Roger Dunsmore, Bill Kittridge, Bill Evans, Louis Welch, Earl Ganz, Maureen Konkle, Dorothy Grow, Patricia Gilliam, Michael Thompson, Joe Sandee, Joe Sand, Joe Haugen, Mike Pryor, David Madsen, Tom Anderson, Gene Nelson, Rene Martell, Dwayne Jaeger, and Ron Harchek.

Here are some folks I met in my travels and process of developing, some of whom I consider family now. The words and support they have given me have been incredible. Thank you to Joy Harjo, Gloria Bird, Robert Conley, Jim Welch, Geary Hobson, Crystos, Vincent Wanasee, Phil RedEagle, Lois Red Elk, Minnie Two Shoes, Charles Courchene, Christopher Coal Miner, Irene Bedard, Ralph Brannen, Gary Farmer, Roberta Whiteman, George C. Wolfe, Loylld Richards, Curt Dempster, Tim Bond, Linda Hartzell, Jane Campbell, Peter Hackett, Tom

Rooney, Steven Wing, Jon Jorgensen, Sean Walbeck, Christina Yao, Martha Brice, Ken Jackson, Jane Kane, the folks at the Crystal Theater in Missoula, Montana (Joel and Jacye), and a whole lot of other folks. One last time, thank you.

PERFORMANCE HISTORY

The Star Quilter

This play, written in 1987, was first presented in a staged reading at the Crystal Theatre in Missoula, Montana, under the direction of William S. Yellow Robe, Jr., in 1988. Featured in the cast were:

Mona Grey—LuAnne Smith (Salish-Kootenai)
LuAnne Jorgensen—Willamina (Billie) Gray

The Star Quilter was produced in a radio broadcast by the British Broadcasting Corporation in their *Radio Drama* series in the summer of 1996.

The New Jersey Repertory Theatre Company (NJRep) presented the play, directed by William S. Yellow Robe, Jr., in a staged reading in Long Branch, New Jersey. The cast featured company members of NJRep, including:

Mona Grey—Lindy Regan
LuAnne Jorgensen—Meryl Harris

The Body Guards

This play was developed at the same time as *Rez Politics*. Both plays were written in the spring of 1997. Like *Rez Politics*, it is in its second draft form. *The Body Guards* was first produced by the Wakiknabe Theater Company in Albuquerque, an intertribal theater company, in a full production in November 1997, directed by Faith Lane. Featured in the cast were:

Skin—Stephan Swimmer (Cherokee)
Bennie Horses—William S. Yellow Robe, Jr. (Assiniboine)

The play had a second production by Wakiknabe in January 1999, when the theater company presented it at the Taos Arts Association, in Taos, New Mexico. Steven Sexton, co-artistic director of Wakiknabe, directed this production. Featured in the cast were:

Skin—William S. Yellow Robe, Jr. (Assiniboine)
Bennie Horses—Duane Schrock (Santa Domingo Pueblo/Kiowa)

On May 24, 1999, NJRep presented a staged reading of *The Body Guards* on a double bill with *The Star Quilter*. The staged readings, directed by William S. Yellow Robe, Jr., took place at the home of NJRep in Long Branch. Featured in the cast were:

Skin—Brian O'Halloran
Benny—George Eric

Rez Politics

Rez Politics is based on a story from a collection of short stories developed by William S. Yellow Robe, Jr., called *Things I Meant to Tell You Later*. It is the first of two short stories Yellow Robe adapted for the stage.

Rez Politics was written in the spring of 1997 and first presented in the summer of the same year in a play-reading series sponsored by the Wakiknabe Theater Company in Albuquerque. The play was directed by associate artistic director Linden Gilbert. Featured in the cast were:

Curtis—Brian Lush (Sioux)
Gerald—William S. Yellow Robe, Jr. (Assiniboine)

Wakiknabe later produced the play, directed by Faith Lane, in a full production in Albuquerque. Featured in this production were:

Curtis—Stephan Swimmer (Cherokee)
Gerald—William S. Yellow Robe, Jr. (Assiniboine)

The Council

The Council was co-commissioned in 1990 by Linda Hartzell, artistic director of the Seattle Children's Theatre, and the late John Kaufman, artistic director of the Honolulu Theatre for Youth, and written later that year. The play received a full production by the Seattle Children's Theatre in January 1991. It was later produced in 1992 by the Honolulu Theatre for Youth, under the direction of William S. Yellow Robe, Jr.

The play was most recently produced by the Wakiknabe Theater Company in Albuquerque. Wakiknabe presented the play, under the direction of William S. Yellow Robe, Jr., as part of a children's festival sponsored by the National Museum of the American Indian in New York City in May 1999. Featured in the production were:

Man/Joey/Fire—Lydell Mitchell (Diné)
Woman/Ice Traveler/Whale/Fire—Rhiana Yazzie (Diné)
Tiger/Fish/Whale—Amanda Jo Wauneka (Diné)
Make/Man 3/Wolf—Kent Blansett (United Band of Keetowah)
Whale/Panda Bear/Man 2—Steven Sexton (Pawnee/Choctaw)
Music Director—Roget Cultee (Quinault)

Sneaky

Sneaky was written in 1982 and received a cold reading, under the direction of Peter Hackett, at the Denver Center for the Performing Arts in 1987. In the summer of the same year, under the direction of Phyllis SK Look, a staged reading of the play was given by the Seattle Group Theatre.

Sneaky received its first full production at the New World Theatre, under the direction of the New World's artistic director, Roberta Uno, in October 1987. Featured in the cast were:

Frank Rose—George Whirlwind Soldier (Sioux)
Eldon Rose—Scott Shepard (Mohawk)
Kermit Rose—John Cruz (Hawaiian)
Jack Kence—Sven (Stevens)

Sneaky also received a staged reading at the Joe Papp's Public Theatre/New York Shakespeare Festival Theatre in the spring of 1995. After this reading the play was restructured.

The Wakiknabe Theater Company produced the play twice with three different casts. In the fall of 1998 co-artistic director Rhiana Yazzie directed the play with the following cast:

Frank Rose—Steven Sexton (Pawnee/Choctaw)
Eldon Rose—William S. Yellow Robe, Jr. (Assiniboine)
Kermit Rose—Ron Harnage (Georgia Cherokee)
Jack Kence—Kent Blansett (United Band of Keetowah)

The last known production of the play was by Wakiknabe in January 1999 at the Taos Arts Association in Taos, New Mexico. The play was directed by Rhiana Yazzie. Featured in the cast of this production were:

Frank Rose—Steven Sexton (Pawnee/Choctaw)
Eldon Rose—Duane Schrock (Santa Domingo Pueblo/Kiowa)
Kermit Rose—William S. Yellow Robe, Jr. (Assiniboine)
Jack Kence—Kent Blansett (United Band of Keetowah).

where the pavement ends

The Star Quilter

A PLAY IN ONE ACT

This one-act play is dedicated to my mother,
Ms. Mina Rose Forest-Yellowrobe.

Characters

MONA GRAY: At the beginning of the play she is a woman in her mid-thirties. She is a Native American. Her kids are at school, some attending boarding school. Her husband works as a carpenter. As the play progresses, she ages.

LUANNE JORGENSEN: At the beginning of the play she is also in her mid-thirties. She is a second-generation Montana farmer whose family came to the state in the 1920s. She is one of three children and has two children of her own.

SCENE ONE

PLACE: The home of Mona Gray. The action takes place in her living room.

TIME: late 1960s, in the fall, on a weekday.

Mona Gray is sitting in an old wooden folding chair near her bed. She is wearing a handmade dress and a long apron. Her hair is in two long braids. Her living room also serves as her bedroom. An old black-and-white television set sits on top of a dresser, and an old star quilt covers a couch. There are pictures and clay reliefs of American Indians on the wall.

At the sound of a car Mona looks up, waits, and then returns to her sewing. There is the sound of a car door shutting, followed by footsteps.

LuAnne Jorgensen enters. She is a small woman wearing a nice store-bought coat and carrying a black purse. She stops at the doorway of the living room.

LUANNE

Uh, hello. Is anybody—oh! Hello.

Mona is surprised and gets to her feet.

MONA

Hello.

LUANNE

You must be Mona—Mona Gray?

MONA

I know that. Who are you?

LUANNE

Why, everyone knows me. I'm LuAnne Jorgensen. Justin Jorgensen's wife.

She giggles and walks into the room.

MONA

Oh yes, I know you. You're JJ's wife.

LUANNE

Uh-huh. That's exactly right. Everybody knows my husband, JJ. He's quite the character. People told me he used to carry on like a wild Indian before I tamed him and married him. He still likes to eat out of the fridge, but you know how men are?

MONA

Well, I heard a car drive up, but I thought it was my cousin Phillip.

LUANNE

Oh. I'm so sorry. I was told it would be all right if I just walked right in. I mean, that's what JJ told me.

MONA

Really bold—I guess you are JJ's wife.

LUANNE

I'm not from here like JJ, so I didn't know. I was born and raised around Brockway, where we don't have Indians.

MONA

They must lock their doors, enit? I was raised around the Sioux, Gros Ventures, and a few Cree, but we always knocked before entering someone's home.

LUANNE

Well, it was just a mistake.

MONA

Did you close the door, or is it still open?

LUANNE

Oh yes, I did do that. Could I sit down?

MONA

Yes. Sit there, on the couch.

LUANNE

It's so good to finally meet you. I've heard so much about you.

MONA

Oh. I hope it was good. From who?

LUANNE

Oh, you know, from different people you meet in town. They told me to come and see you.

MONA

About what?

LUANNE

Oh, it's something a few of the ladies in town are doing. Say—this is a lovely home. This isn't one of those free homes your people are supposed to get, is it?

MONA

This house? No, this is a good house. It used to be part of the old hospital. I had the money, so I went and bought it.

LUANNE

It's really nice. I love those clay—yes, clay—pictures on the walls. How many of you are there? I mean, who lives here?

MONA

Oh, just my family. No one else. Why?

LUANNE

With all your family, it seems kind of small.

MONA

We like it. It's our home.

LUANNE

You should see our home. JJ—uh, Justin built it new just for me and the boys, a real nice place just twenty miles north of town, but being that winter is moving in, we're staying in Justin's parents' old house in town. If you were to see it, I know you'd just love it.

MONA

Oh. Good for you folks.

LUANNE

You know, I think it's really odd. You people get to vote in our elections. But we don't get to vote in your—what do you call them? "Tribal" elections?

MONA

LuAnne, up until 1954, we Indin people didn't get to vote in "your" elections. We weren't even considered citizens in our country until 1924. Our tribal elections decide who rules the roost on the reservation. You can vote if you're an enrolled Indin. White people have the option of voting with their feet. We lost our moccasins a long time ago.

LUANNE

Mona. You lost me. I don't know what you're talking about.

MONA

Don't be offended, but the fact is, if a non-Indian doesn't like the policies set by Indins on the reservation, they can leave, but we have nowhere else to go, to feel like ourselves. Excuse me again, LuAnne, but aren't you part Indin?

LUANNE

Me? No. Of course not. We're white. I'm white. My whole family is white. Well, my grandfather was German and my grandmother was English, but no, we don't have any Indian blood in us at all.

MONA

But I thought your grandfather was a cousin to Silas Henderson.

LUANNE

Silas? No!

MONA

Yes, Silas was supposed to be a half-breed. JJ's uncle.

LUANNE

That might be true of JJ, but not my side of the family. We're real Americans. Fourth-generation Montanans.

MONA

Are you sure?

LUANNE

Of course I'm sure. We would know if something like that was true.

MONA

Don't get upset, Mrs. Jorgensen, but you never can be too sure. Besides, I don't put up with too much gossip.

LUANNE

I don't either.

MONA

Would you like some tea and bannock?

LUANNE

Just some tea please, no—uh—"bansock" for me.

MONA

JJ really likes bannock. He used to eat it all the time when he was with us.

LUANNE

He did?

MONA

Sure did. He likes his with a lot of grease on it.

LUANNE

Uh, I'm here because we—the ladies of the Elks—want to give Senator Feltcher something special when he comes to town. Something he can take back to Washington.

MONA

I thought they already gave him a cowboy hat. One of those big black ones with a big feather and a silver band around it? At least, that's what I read in the newspaper.

LUANNE

We have, but we want something that's different from all the other western states' senators.

MONA

Well, you know, different ones tell about when President Coolidge came to Montana. Some Indin people gave him a headdress one time. I don't remember what tribe it was, but they gave it to him. Is that what you want for this man?

LUANNE

Oh no, no. Nothing that cliché, but somehow, yes, maybe something along those lines. Something, you know, something your people would have?

MONA

A block of cheese?

LUANNE

Yes—no. Oh, no, don't be silly.

MONA

I know. I have an old dancing outfit I used to wear—oh, I know. I make dancing outfits for my children, but only for my relatives, no one else. I guess that's not a good idea. Most of the celebrations are over now, and I don't know who could make you one on such short notice. They really make them fancy nowadays.

LUANNE

No, no—not a dancing costume. We were thinking, well, we've heard you make star quilts. We'd like you to make a star quilt for the senator. He could take it back to Washington with him and display it in his office. Something that people, when they see it, they'll know he's from Montana.

MONA

You want me to sew a star quilt for him?

LUANNE

We're willing to pay you.

MONA

I don't know.

LUANNE

We wouldn't dream of asking you to make it for free or donating it. I'm the chairwoman of the committee, and I can write a check for it. I see you're working on one now.

LuAnne gets to her feet, crosses over to the bed, and looks at the star quilt.

My. It's gorgeous.

MONA

Thank you.

LUANNE

It's beautiful. How do you do it?

MONA

I just learned to do it. It helps bring in money for what we need. Will—that's my husband—he has times when he isn't working, and then this brings some extra money into the house when things get tight.

LUANNE

I just love the colors.

MONA

I use one color, and then all its shades. They all flow towards the center point.

LUANNE

Uh, Mona?

MONA

Mrs. Jorgensen, this quilt is not for sale.

LUANNE

Why not? Mona, I can give you a check right now. The check is good. I know—I can make it out to myself, take it to the bank, cash it, and then bring you the money. How's that?

MONA

This star quilt is a gift for someone.

LUANNE

If you don't want a check, I can get you the cash. We weren't sure you had a checking account. I hear it's hard to cash a check if you don't have an account.

MONA

No, it isn't the check.

LUANNE

Well then, how much would it cost us to buy this one?

MONA

This one isn't for sale.

LUANNE

Why not?

MONA

This is for my nephew's giveaway.

LUANNE

Give a what?

MONA

It's a ceremony we have.

LUANNE

Oh! A ceremony! This is a ceremonial blanket? That would make it even better if the senator was to receive this one. It's so pretty.

MONA

This star quilt is special.

LUANNE

Let me say one thing, Mona.

MONA

This one is for my nephew.

LUANNE

The senator would really cherish this star quilt if he knew it was a ceremonial blanket. Did I mention the presentation of the blanket will be at the Elks Lodge? You could come if you want. It's a fifty-dollar-a-plate bean dinner to help raise money for his upcoming campaign. You could come and watch as we present it to him.

MONA

Mrs. Jorgensen, you must not be hearing me right. I said this quilt is not for sale.

LUANNE

Now, now—don't get upset, Mona. There is nothing to get riled about. Maybe it doesn't have to be this blanket. Could you make another quilt for us?

MONA

I don't know. When do you need it?

LUANNE

In about three weeks. We only want one blanket for the senator. It shouldn't be hard for you to make. We've heard you've been making these quilts for a long time.

MONA

I don't even know this man.

LUANNE

Here.

Reaches into her purse and removes a brochure.

MONA

It would be easier for me . . .

LUANNE

Here. This is one of the senator's campaign brochures. It talks a little about the senator, his family, their history, and what he wants to do for Montana. Please take it and read it. I have plenty more.

MONA

I'll have to ask my husband first, and then we'll see.

LUANNE

Thank you, but we don't have much time.

MONA

I thought you said you wanted the quilt in three weeks?

LUANNE

I'll pay you whatever you want for it.

MONA

I still don't know. I usually don't make them and sell them like the stores do. I only do it when we are really down and out or if it's for someone in the family, one of our relatives.

LUANNE

Who did you say you were making this one for?

MONA

My nephew's giveaway. He doesn't even know I'm making it for him. It'll be a big surprise.

LUANNE

Then he wouldn't know if you sold it.

MONA

No, I don't think so. I can't sell you this one.

LUANNE

But it's such a beautiful blanket. The senator would have loved this one.

MONA

You really like this man, Mrs. Jorgensen?

LUANNE

Oh, yes, he's a very good man. He's done a lot for Montana and he's going for his third term. I've even met his wife, Wendy, and their kids, Bobby and Jimmy. We ate dinner with them at the Custer Hotel.

MONA

I won't sell you this one. But . . .

LUANNE

But—but you'll make another one for him? Would you?

MONA

I suppose I could. I'll need some more materials. Thread, cloth, cotton batting, and some chalk to mark it with.

LUANNE

This is so wonderful. How much do you think it will cost?

MONA

It won't be much. Say, twenty dollars for the materials. I have to buy cotton at the store, and that usually runs more then the other materials I use. It might be over thirty dollars when I get done. Then I always ask for some money for myself for the work I do.

LUANNE

Really? How much? One, two, three hundred dollars?

MONA

No, no. I'll charge you what I usually charge most people. It would come out to be eighty dollars, altogether.

LUANNE

Why that's cheaper than the hat we bought him last time. This is so wonderful, Mona. I'm really happy I stopped here. Be sure to read the brochure. And you can have the blanket finished in three weeks?

MONA

After I finish this one, I'll start his.

LUANNE

That's just wonderful. I'll leave you my telephone number where you can reach me. You do have a telephone, don't you?

MONA

I keep it unlisted.

LUANNE

Yes. Well, should I leave part of the money now?

MONA

I thought you were going to pay me all of it now. But part will be all right, I suppose.

LUANNE

Thank you, Mona. Oh, thank you. Here. I'll need a receipt.

She reaches into her purse and removes some money.

Here—here's thirty dollars.

MONA

Thank you.

They exchange the receipt. LuAnne checks it and puts it into her purse.

Good-bye.

LUANNE

Good-bye. As JJ would say, "have to make some dust."

She exits. Mona watches her. Sound of a car. Mona begins to read the brochure.

MONA

"A man for all Montanans. For the farmers, ranchers, businessmen, and just plain regular 'Montana' folks." Hmmm. I wonder if he thinks Indin people are just plain, or just regular.

Blackout.

SCENE TWO

TIME: Early 1970s, in the spring, on a weekday.

Mona is at work on a different quilt. She is very quiet. LuAnne is sitting on the couch, is smoking a cigarette and drinking coffee.

LUANNE

And the senator was telling all of us how awful some of the events were in Washington, D.C. during all the marches and riots. He and his lovely wife were just completely surrounded with long-haired good-for-nothing people and coloreds, carrying signs, screaming and yelling. Then Justin says, "Why Senator, you're a fourth-generation, Montanan. That sounds like the old western days with the Indians. It shouldn't have bothered you." Well, we all laughed so hard. Some of the people who were near our table broke up when they heard Justin. He can be such a card.

MONA

I'll bet he is.

LUANNE

I guess you had to be there. But you know, Mona, I did tell him one thing. It's so sad about how all the young people are acting up, and then the coloreds. All the marches and protesting are slowly coming to a halt. It's just wonderful none of our Indians here in Montana did any of that marching stuff, or protesting. It's like we have an unwritten agreement that both people understand. Sort of an order to things. That's what I said. I made sure everyone in that restaurant in Billings—at the Custer Hotel, mind you—heard me. I said, "At least our Indians behave."

MONA

Did anyone say anything about Wounded Knee? How those Indians took over that town. Did anyone say anything about that?

LUANNE

No, because that was in South Dakota. It wasn't any of our Indians here in Montana.

MONA

What about your Senator Fletcher? Did he have anything to say about that?

LUANNE

No, he didn't. It was South Dakota. They're just as bad as those North Dakotans. Reminds me of a little joke I heard. There was this North Dakotan . . .

MONA

We heard a lot of things about Wounded Knee. A lot of young people started to ask questions. They were the same questions we've been wondering about for a long time. It made Will and the council think, too. What if it happened here?

LUANNE

Oh, Mona, it wasn't as bad as the press made it . . .

MONA

How do you know? Were you there?

LUANNE

No, but I read the newspapers like everyone else.

MONA

Maybe you don't read the same newspapers.

LUANNE

Oh now, what's that supposed to mean? We're both from the same area. We travel the same streets as one another. Our husbands are from this area, too. We're both Montanans.

MONA

Oh? I'm an Assiniboine first, long before there was a Montana. I don't know sometimes.

LUANNE

Well, you saw the *Gazette*. The pictures they carried of the protest. All those young long-haired Indian men, holding weapons and burning the flag. It was just disgraceful. Not one of our Indians was there, I can promise you that.

MONA

You'd be surprised about the number of things you don't know.

LUANNE

Oh? What does that mean? Mona? Was there someone from here who was over there? Is that what you're saying?

MONA

I didn't say anything.

LUANNE

Oh, please tell me, Mona. Who was it? Someone from the Stryker family? I bet it was one of those boys. They used to drive around in the country at night stealing the batteries from the tractors. Are they Indian?

MONA

Yes, even though they don't have dark skin, but their hearts are. They're breeds—and no, it wasn't them.

LUANNE

They are Indian, huh? They don't look it. I always thought they were poor white trash. But—but who was it, Mona? Who was over there from here?

MONA

I thought you knew everything because you read it in the newspapers?

LUANNE

Well, no one will ever know what really happened inside that town. And there is no way something like that will ever happen here in Montana. We all get along, because we know where each other belongs. And as far as who, if anybody, was involved from here, I'll find out eventually. You know how small this town is. Word will get out, and half the town will know about it.

MONA

Part of this town already knows.

LUANNE

Oh? Oh, I see what you're getting at. Half the Indian part of town knows about it. Is that what you're trying to say?

MONA

I didn't say that.

LUANNE

But that's what you meant, isn't it?

MONA

In a way, I guess I did.

LUANNE

Well, if it is, . . . was, . . . so important, I'm sure the young man's name will appear in the Gazette by tomorrow morning, when it gets around. If it really means something.

MONA

But aren't you—you know, curious? About why all that happened—and of all the times, too? Things are starting to change. I remember at one time we used to have signs hangin' up, like—"No dogs or Indians allowed." And what happened at Wounded Knee is sort of like the olden days.

LUANNE

Oh, now you're over exaggerating things. People would never do something like that here in Montana.

MONA

Yes they did. In some areas. Now the signs are gone, but the looks on people's faces are still there.

LUANNE

You just want to make the newspapers. But I will say one thing, it was sad because a lot of people in that town lost a lot of valuable belongings.

MONA

Both times.

LUANNE

What?

MONA

I don't mean to get you angry, LuAnne. Say—how does the Senator like his star quilt?

LUANNE

Oh yes—that's right. He loves it. He still hangs it on the wall at his office.

MONA

On the wall of his office? I thought he was going to use it for their bed.

LUANNE

Oh no, Mona. It was to show how much he cares for all the people of Montana.

MONA

When I make something like that for someone, I put something special into it, to help that person. Does your senator look at it?

LUANNE

I don't know that, Mona. I don't travel to Washington, D.C., all the time. Honestly.

MONA

Will and some of my relations were mad at me for making that quilt. Will got mad and then he wanted me to make one for the man who ran against your senator.

LUANNE

I wondered where Joe Hopkins got his hands on a star quilt. It was you?

MONA

Yes. Will and the tribal board thought it would be fair if I made him one too. That way they wouldn't have so much trouble, no matter who won.

LUANNE

Getting into a little politicking, eh, Mona? That's so sweet.

MONA

I don't really mind. I didn't know those two men. It was my husband and relatives who worried me, though.

LUANNE

Is that the reason for your latest creation there?

MONA

This? No. It's for a friend of my son. He and some other people are trying to raise money, so they asked me if I would make one so they could raffle it off.

LUANNE

Oh. It looks beautiful, as always.

MONA

Yes. And it's not for sale.

LUANNE

I wasn't asking.

MONA

I didn't mean it like that, LuAnne.

LUANNE

But it sounded like it. I didn't come here to try and get another star quilt from you. There are other women who make star quilts, you know.

MONA

Ah, I know. I told you some of their names. And they came here and told me you went to see them.

LUANNE

Oh. About my little project?

MONA

Yes.

LUANNE

I suppose you were a little jealous that I didn't ask you first?

MONA

No, I'm not jealous. It sounds interesting, but I don't mind if I'm not involved. I have a lot of things around here that will keep me busy for a long time.

LUANNE

Not even a little? Oh come on, now. I bet you were a little upset about the possibility of being left out?

MONA

No. Why should I be?

LUANNE

Because you knew I would be saving the best for last?

MONA

What?

LUANNE

Well, what do you think of my little project?

MONA

Do you really want to know the truth, LuAnne?

LUANNE

Sure. I've never been afraid to take praise when it was due.

MONA

Well, a few days ago, different women were coming here to my house and told me that you came to their house asking them if they made star quilts and that you were going to make a business for them. I didn't mind that at all. In fact some of the women really liked the idea. Sophia Shelter really likes it, because her and her husband don't have a lot of money. It's hard for her husband, Benny, to find work. I felt good about that, but—but what I didn't like, or was kind of upset about, was the fact you went and told these women I knew you. You told them that I said it was okay for this business project to happen. When you asked me for those names, I didn't know you were going to go and see those people. You just asked me for names. Will was very upset, too. He told me, I talk to you too much.

LUANNE

Will was mad? He of all people should appreciate what I'm trying to do. He's probably jealous that it's a woman who came up with the idea.

MONA

Not just Will, but like I said, I was more than a little upset, too. I wouldn't have given you their names if I'd known you would be that gull-pushy.

LUANNE

Oh, Mona. You're just getting over the fact that I didn't ask you first is all.

MONA

No, I'm not. I just told you why. I . . .

LUANNE

Come on now, Mona—I heard what you said. I know what's going on in your mind. I bet you thought I would leave you out.

MONA

Whatever.

LUANNE

But with all that aside, what do you'really think of the idea?

MONA

What? Haven't you been listening, LuAnne? I just said—oh, never mind.

LUANNE

Let me explain it to you. What I wanted to do was to hire all your friends and have all of you make star quilts. I'll take the star quilts you make and sell them back east—say, New York—and then even the west coast, like Los Angeles. And, whatever money we make, we'll split it among everyone. No one will be left out.

MONA

Who—who would want to buy a star quilt in those big cities?

LUANNE

What? What do you mean?

MONA

If they wanted one, they could come here and hang around. Who knows? Someone might want to be friends with them and give them one for free.

LUANNE

That's not the point, though, Mona. No one will come out here.

MONA

Why not? If they have the money to buy a quilt, they could afford gas money to come out here.

LUANNE

Well, some of those people in the bigger cities don't really know what it's like out here. People are afraid to come out here now. They think white people aren't allowed on the reservations.

MONA

Who told them that, I suppose? And here you are, just sitting here, talking with me.

LUANNE

When we were in Washington, D.C., we were at a party and some folks came up and asked that very question. "Are white people allowed on the reservations?"

MONA

What did you say? Did you tell them the truth?

LUANNE

Of course I did. I told them in Montana they are. But this person who asked the question then told us he has a cousin who lives in Minnesota. And they said they have a reservation in their state that doesn't allow white people to live on it.

MONA

Oh my—really? Did he say where this was?

LUANNE

Minnesota.

MONA

What tribe?

LUANNE

What?

MONA

What Indin tribe?

LUANNE

I don't really remember what tribe he said. He wasn't too sure himself. He said it sounded like "chippy, chippy" something.

MONA

Oh. Then how do they know about star quilts and don't even know what Indian tribe is near them?

LUANNE

Because Senator Feltcher displays his star quilt and he gets a lot of questions about it.

MONA

Oh. I see.

LUANNE

And because of this, I want to start this business. There are a lot of people who want a blanket just like the senator's. I think all of us could really make a profit from this. And all you Indian ladies have to do is keep doing what you do best, making star quilts.

MONA

But that's not all we do. We have a lot of other things we have to do, just for our families.

LUANNE

I know, but what woman doesn't? You see, Mona, first of all we have all of you ladies work on making star quilts. Then you give them to me. I'll package them with the help of my son and send them to a friend of ours in New York. He'll sell them and send money back to us. We'll take the money and split it among you Indian ladies.

MONA

Who is this friend of yours?

LUANNE

Oh, don't worry about him.

MONA

And you'll pay for all the materials we use?

LUANNE

Not all of it at first. Just a percentage to get started. We'll all have to pitch in a little at first.

MONA

What about your friend? Is he going to pitch in a little, too?

LUANNE

He already has. He's doing the advertising. He's already come up with a name for the company.

MONA

Company? What kind of name are you going to use?

LUANNE

"Princess Light Sleeps" quilts.

MONA

Oh. Who's that?

LUANNE

Who's who?

MONA

This Princess Light Sleeps—she a Canadian?

LUANNE

It's just a name. It's a made-up Indian name.

MONA

I guess it is.

LUANNE

What do you think, Mona?

MONA

Did you know some of the women who will be making these star quilts are not only Assiniboine but Sioux as well?

LUANNE

Yes—oh, yes—Ass-sinny-boing and Sioux.

MONA

Assiniboine.

LUANNE

Yes. Whatever, Mona. That's why we're calling it the Princess Light Sleeps company. People can pronounce it easier. Mona, do you want to become a part of this business or not?

MONA

Well, you do have some women who do very good work. I don't really see why you need me.

LUANNE

Because you're my friend. You helped give me the idea.

MONA

I don't know. I think you should let me think about this one first. Not like the last time.

LUANNE

A lot of your friends are excited about it. You won't be working in a building like a regular company, but out of your homes. You'll have a chance to visit each other and work at each other's house.

MONA

And these other women, do they like it?

LUANNE

Yes—oh, yes.

MONA

I—I suppose so.

LUANNE

You mean you'll do it?

MONA

Yes.

LUANNE

Well, then I better go and get things started. I have a lot of things to do.

MONA

I have a lot of work to do myself. Let me know what all happens.

LUANNE

I will, I will.

MONA

All these women really want to do this, huh? What a thing to do. It's going to be a big project. Could be a real good business. Maybe later we could sell our beadwork the same way.

LuAnne begins to exit.

LUANNE

Yes. Yes, it is wonderful. Feel good about it. You have a lot of influence, Mona. Most of the women were waiting to hear you say you'd be a part of it before they would do it. Good-bye.

She exits. Mona has a look of horror on her face. Blackout.

SCENE THREE

TIME: Mid-1980s, in the summer, on a weekday.

Mona is folding a star quilt. Near her is a large plastic garbage bag. She makes a final inspection of the quilt. She hears the sound of a car, goes to a window and looks out, then hurries toward the door.

MONA

Oh no. Oh no.

We hear LuAnne from off stage.

LUANNE

Mona? Mona? Are you home?

Mona is standing near the doorway.

MONA

Yes, but I don't think you should come into the house.

LUANNE

What? I don't see a sign saying, "White people not allowed." Besides, I thought we were friends?

MONA

You never get things right. I don't think it would be good for us to visit today. I'm tired today anyway, and my face will show that . . .and a lot of other things, too.

LUANNE

I just want to say something. Just for a few minutes, at least.

Mona stands for a moment and then backs away from the door way. LuAnne enters the house.

MONA

I suppose it would be all right if we just visit, but not too long.

LUANNE

I see you finally took up the habit of locking your door. We have, too.

MONA

Things have gotten worse since Reagan took office.

LUANNE

Oh, we can't blame that on the president. Oh, say—that looks nice. I hear Will is doing his third term on the tribal board now. You shouldn't complain.

MONA

Well, that's what I mean. Instead of things improving, some are just getting worse. Money is getting hard to come by. Go ahead, sit down and rest.

LUANNE

See—I knew we were still friends. I must be doing something right.

MONA

No, this is common hospitality we have.

LUANNE

We all have it, Mona.

MONA

Have you come to apologize—finally?

LUANNE

For what?

MONA

For the business offer you brought here the last time you came to my house.

LUANNE

I thought it turned out great for some of us.

MONA

You still don't know what happened, do you?

LUANNE

What are you talking about?

MONA

To this day, some of those women won't talk to me.

LUANNE

Now wait a minute—it wasn't my fault. Those women backed out on us. Left us without even telling us—no letter, not even a phone call. Besides, I took a loss like everyone else.

MONA

They didn't leave you right away. They did work for about two months and made over twenty-five quilts. And you—you, were the only one of us who could afford to take a loss. Especially with that oil well on your land.

LUANNE

If I had known all we were going to do was go over that old business project, I wouldn't have come inside your house.

MONA

I find that hard to believe, since that's all you ever came here to do was some bad business project.

LUANNE

It really wasn't my fault. How was I to know the man in New York was selling the star quilts for over eight hundred dollars a piece? It took me two months before I found out.

MONA

And then, we heard you were trying to get a share of that money for yourself. Your son was the one who accidentally told us when he came to pick up the quilts that day. Because you couldn't do it, because you were on the phone talking with that man. And then you came to my house and tried to make it sound like you were doing it for us.

LUANNE

But you knew yourself. Somehow, you got word.

MONA

It was Will's cousin who was working at the BIA in Washington, D.C., who called Will and told him. I couldn't believe I had those women working for only a small amount. Did you know, LuAnne, that some of them were actually hocking their belongings to buy thread just so they could stay in your little project. Some of those women bought up large amounts of material and were left holding the bag, because their families went without. And here, when it came down to it, the large amounts were never going to come our way. I didn't want to believe it at first. It really shamed me out.

LUANNE

It wasn't your fault.

MONA

In a way, it was. I did something I shouldn't have done.

LUANNE

Well, I look back and the old saying comes back to me. Ignorance is bliss.

MONA

My people have never seen stupidity as an honorable thing.

LUANNE

There you go again. Breaking it down into an issue of race. Race has nothing to do with it. We were just a bunch of country bumpkins who were taken in by a city slicker.

MONA

I suppose that's one way of looking at it, but we were the ones who did most of the work. You had us doing most of the packing as well.

LUANNE

I worked just as hard.

MONA

I guess—I guess you did. You were the only one who could make the long distance telephone calls.

LUANNE

I should leave.

MONA

I won't stop you. I should go have my head examined at IHS whilel I'm at it.

LUANNE

I only wanted to help. And are those other women really still mad about it?

MONA

Yes! We were all surprised when Will was elected. I wasn't kidding about that.

LUANNE

Well, businesses are like that sometimes. No one can predict what will happen. It's that way in a lot of other businesses. Not just us. Say—I understand that some of those new council members get new houses when they get on the board. Why haven't you gotten one?

MONA

If Indin people were to get all these free things like you've heard, we could all be millionaires and there wouldn't be any reservations. We could buy land and start our own countries. LuAnne, this is my house. I bought it. Me. I bought it with money I made from leasing my land to a farmer. Do you think I stole this house? Oh dear. Why did you come here?

LUANNE

Now there isn't any need to get upset Mona. It's like I said. I'm just here for a visit. And yes, I'm a little sorry for what happened.

MONA

You say that every time, but I don't know if your tongue, brain, and heart are connected.

LUANNE

What? That's funny, isn't it? I guess, that's how you and me are supposed to work things out. But when it comes down to it, Mona, even though you're an Indian, you've always been a good friend to me. Oh—I see you're making a new quilt.

MONA

No, I just finished it. I'm getting ready to take it over to the community hall. My niece is coming to pick me up in an hour or so.

LUANNE

Really? Who is this one for?

MONA

You don't know her. No one really did.

LUANNE

Someone local?

MONA

Yes. Cheryl Horse. One of my granddaughters from Poplar.

LUANNE

Oh. Is this one of those give-a-something blankets?

MONA

No, it's for her . . . her burial.

LUANNE

Oh, Mona—oh, my dear. I didn't know. I'm so sorry to hear it. How did she—how did she pass away? Here, sit down. You poor thing.

MONA

Her mother and aunty, they were coming to Wolf Point. They were waiting to get on the highway and a drunk driver swerved and slammed his car into their car. Her mother and aunty were the only ones, who . . .

LUANNE

Oh, Mona, I'm so sorry. Really—I'm so sorry to hear it.

MONA

Cheryl, she was my boy's youngest daughter. His only girl. I was going to name her this summer. I was going to name her after my grandmother. I was planning to make a whole bunch of quilts for her. This little one. They—my boy, her parents—asked me if I would do the naming ceremony for them. Now, instead of doing that they want something to put on the coffin. This is the last one for me. I'm going to quit making quilts after this one.

LUANNE

I'm sorry to hear it.

MONA

She was so young. Too young to leave this world.

LUANNE

I know how you feel. We lost a grandson of ours not long ago.

MONA

Yes—I remember now. Oh, I'm sorry, LuAnne.

LUANNE

Kyle was visiting us and wanted to ride horses. He was doing fine, until the horse hit a gopher's hole and threw him. JJ took it harder than I expected. His mother was still young and so was our boy. They didn't know what to do, so I had to make all the arrangements. Just like you're doing now. So many changes . . . between us, I've always wondered if we're getting closer, or just growing further apart?

MONA

It's always that way with people. Just when you think you know, something happens.

LUANNE

Mona, I know this is a bad time for you. I have to be honest with you. There was another reason why I came here. Now, I don't think I could ask you. It doesn't seem like the right thing to do now. I was going to ask you—ask you . . .

MONA

No. No, LuAnne. I can't do it any more. My eyes are really bad. The doctors say I have diabetes. I might loose my sight if I don't quit. And even then, I just told you, I quit. I can't go back now.

LUANNE

You knew? How—how did you know what I was going to ask you when I never said a word?

MONA

Leave. Quick. Hurry up. Please don't say any more, LuAnne. Today is a bad day for me. Don't press me like you always do. I'm afraid.

LUANNE

Afraid? What? Listen to yourself.

MONA

I'm afraid of what I might do or say. Listen to me. Today is a very bad day for me. I don't know what I'm going to do. So please don't say any more.

LUANNE

I—I understand.

LuAnne gets to her feet and exits.

MONA

This time, I hope you do.

Blackout.

SCENE FOUR

TIME: 1992, winter, on a weekday.

Mona sits on her bed. She has an old star quilt wrapped around her shoulders and she is holding a star-quilt pattern in her hands. She feels along the stitching of the pattern. We hear the sound of a car stopping, then footsteps. LuAnne stands in the doorway.

LUANNE

Hello. Is anyone home?

MONA

Why is it, I believe, that would never stop you?

LUANNE

Mona? How are you, dear?

MONA

Fine. I'm fine. I'm feeling good today and I thought you might be stopping by. I haven't heard from you in a long time.

LUANNE

I'm—I'm sorry to hear about Will. He was a good politician, wasn't he?

MONA

Yes. Will was a good man. I miss him now and then. I thought I would follow him, but who knows. How is Justin?

LUANNE

Mean as ever. He's getting into politics himself. He wants to run for the state house of representatives.

MONA

Do you think he'll win?

LUANNE

I don't think he will. I think he knows it too, but it's something he's always wanted to do. Justin wants to play politician now. He would never have thought like this twenty years ago.

MONA

Are you campaigning for him now?

LUANNE

No. He couldn't pay me to do that. He could afford it, though. They've discovered a third well on his land.

MONA

I remember traveling with Will all around the reservation. Passing out cards and visiting with people. I didn't mind it. It was a chance for me to visit relatives I didn't see too often.

LUANNE

Yes. You know how men are.

MONA

No shame. Some of them have no shame at all.

LUANNE

You've been keeping yourself busy—that's good. I see you're still making star quilts. No one could match your work, Mona— that's a fact.

MONA

My niece would be jealous if she heard you say that, LuAnne. This isn't mine. No. I wish I could, but I can't.

LUANNE

Well, what is it that you've got a hold of there in your hands, Mona? Eh?

MONA

You've been away for a long time, LuAnne. Everyone else knows why but you. I'm—I can't see.

LUANNE

What? Oh, my . . .

MONA

It's the diabetes. I lost my sight over two years ago. My niece, Kim, comes to the house to take care of me. I haven't sewn in a long time. This is some of her work.

She doesn't even know I have it. I'm surprised no one has told you.

LUANNE

I haven't been out and about as much as I used to. I'm so sorry, Mona. I would never imagine you getting that disease. You were always working. Even now, look at you. It makes me feel so sad.

MONA

So am I, but just a little—not a lot. In a way, I kind of feel lucky. You should see how diabetes affects others. Kim—she just started this pattern today. I thought I'd feel it over and find out how she's coming along on it.

LUANNE

Well, I'm glad that someone is looking out for you. I haven't seen one of my relatives in a long time. Now I know why our parents were thankful for the holidays.

MONA

Oh, there are a lot of people who come and check in to see how I'm making it through the day.

LUANNE

In thirty years, Mona, I still haven't come across a person who matches your work. It seems you are the only one I know who knows what quality is. I came here to ask you for a favor again. Now, I don't even know how I can do it. It seemed so easy, but now . . .

MONA

What's wrong, LuAnne? Oh—it's one of *those* visits again.

LUANNE

Mona, JJ is going to be having a campaign rally at the Elks. I wanted something to have in the background, and—and you are the only one I know.

MONA

The only Indin you know.

LUANNE

No. That isn't true, Mona. I need your help, and I came to you because I would rather turn to a friend instead of a stranger. And that is a mean thing to say to me, Mona. After all these years.

MONA

LuAnne, why haven't you asked one of those other women who used to work with us on that project. You know why? They won't even answer their door when you come. I know. It's the truth. But really, LuAnne, when you come down to it, what I'm saying to you now, and comparing it to some of the other things you said to me when we first met, it really isn't. Have you ever learned to say the name of my people correctly after all these years?

LUANNE

Why yes. "Assiniboine." It took me forever, but I learned it. As a friend, it was the least I could do.

MONA

That's good to hear.

LUANNE

You have to remember that not a lot of people have heard of your tribe before. After the first day I met with some of the ladies of the Elks, and even though they have been here with their families for years, some of them have never heard of your tribe. Isn't that funny? We know the name of every cow from our herds but don't even know the proper names of our neighbors.

MONA

And if they have never heard of the Assiniboine, we never existed. It seems to be like that for all Indin people. Moo.

They both laugh.

I wish it wasn't true, but it is. It reminds me of the time when my boy was in school. He came back and asked me if "Indin" people were around before Columbus, or did Columbus get here first and then we came? It doesn't seem to mean anything at the schools, or in this country, until a white person does it, or knows it. And until that happens, it seems we get pushed aside.

LUANNE

Mona, why are you talking like this? You never used to talk like this before.

MONA

I never did, because I didn't want to get into trouble. When you first came here, I thought you were from the BIA. If I didn't treat you right, I thought you would take away my kids. And as years went along, well, I didn't want hurt you. I would see the hurt in your face, but now I'm old. I can say what I want.

LUANNE

That's my point, Mona. I don't know what you're talking about. Here we are, sharing the same country, shopping at the same stores, buying the same foods, but not eating the same foods. I still, to this day, can't get used to the idea of eating ban-nock.

MONA

You know what, LuAnne? I just realized everything in this world is hidden from me. I can't see it anymore. So why tell a lie and hide the truth about how I feel and what I think? Hiding it, especially from myself? I can't see the hurt in people's faces anymore, but being blind has taught me something else. I can feel the pain. Even my own. You know what's really funny though? This morning, I was washing my hands, and for the first time, I could feel my knuckles and how swollen they've become. I could feel my fingers ache from doing all that sewing. When Will couldn't get a job, the house was so cold, even my fingernails ached . . . aye—not that bad. The years are catching up with me. LuAnne, let me ask you something. If it wasn't for wanting that star quilt, would you have ever come to an Indin home, or kept on returning to my house?

LUANNE

What a thing to say.

MONA

I just wanted to know. It's something Will used to tell me all the time. I started to believe it, too.

LUANNE

Stop coming to your house, because you're an Indian? Oh, that's foolish. Wait—that isn't true to a point. I don't know, Mona. I might have, when I—when I couldn't get a quilt. But I have thought of you from time to time.

MONA

Then why didn't you come to visit me when you didn't want a star quilt?

LUANNE

Like I said. I've thought about coming to visit lots of times.

MONA

Then why didn't you?

LUANNE

Because, among our people, we seem to need reasons for everything we do, practical reasons. Something always came up. Remember, I raised kids and worked.

MONA

We all have, LuAnne. And that's the first time you've ever heard me say something like that. I have something I've always wanted to say to you, but I didn't, because I didn't know how you would take it. When you first came here, you just walked right into my house without even knocking. I didn't mind, because I've had other white people do that—even some Indins here do that. But they stop when they realize they've done something wrong. You never asked me why I made star quilts. You were more concerned about how you could get your hands on one. Money wasn't a big thing, because you had money. But with all this, you still never understood, or asked, why I made star quilts.

Pause.

You might not even want to hear this now. When I was young I used to do a lot of beadwork, a long time ago. Then I got my medicine and received something special to work into the quilts. This "job" of yours led me off my path, the right path. Star quilts are beautiful, because they have one color and all the different shades of that color lead them to the center, the heart. That's why I made these quilts—they came from my heart. I wanted to share this gift with people, because it really made different ones happy. How can you sell something that comes from your heart? It has to be given. I told you the very first day, I didn't want to sell you one for your senator. I didn't even know him.

Pause.

You came here today wanting another star quilt. You, just like a lot of other people, imagine we don't understand you. "Look at those Indians, they're different. They dress like us. But they aren't really like us," is what I've heard. That's true, we are different from you. That's why I always tried to help you. I didn't want to let our differences become a barrier. I really wanted to know who and what you were. And that's because we both live here, in this world. Deer, badgers, even a grasshopper will live near one another, though they are not the same, but each is valuable and necessary in completing the circle.

Pause.

I never found out who else you might be, LuAnne, besides what little of that one side of you I saw. And now that I'm older, I realize I don't know you and you don't know me. Not one thing about me. It makes me feel bad to say this to you. I don't have any more star quilts for you. I gave you the last one a long time ago, and you didn't even know it. We've both grown old and pitiful, but pitiful not because we are old—pitiful that we've been here for so long and still don't know anything about one another. And that makes me feel sad.

She gets up and wraps her shawl around LuAnne.

LUANNE

Mona, can we ever be friends? I feel so empty and cold.

MONA

Warm yourself, LuAnne. At least it could be a start.

Blackout.

The Body Guards

A PLAY IN ONE ACT

Characters

BENNY: a man in his late forties.

CLARENCE: a dead man.

SKIN: a man in his early twenties.

PLACE: An old wooden shack.

TIME: Early 1960s, winter.

Two old wooden folding chairs near a wood stove. Skin and Benny are sitting in the two chairs, leaning back, sleeping, and nearly falling over. Clarence, a corpse, is laid out on an old wooden door, propped up on two sawhorses. We hear the sound of gas being released from Clarence's body.

SKIN

Holy shit! What is that?

BENNY

Damn, Skin! What did you do that for? You should've just gone outside. Open the door.

SKIN

It wasn't me! I bet it was you.

BENNY

Me? You! You're the only one I know who really guzzles that cheap wine.

SKIN

Well, open the door.

BENNY

You. You're the one who did it.

SKIN

No. I'll just sit here, then.

BENNY

God—this guy. I'll do it, then. Hey, Skin? How much did they give you for this job?

SKIN

Why?

BENNY

I was just wonder—whew! Boy, it's cold out there.

SKIN

Then shut it.

BENNY

Don't get too bossy, hey. I'm doing you a favor, airing you and that guy out.

SKIN

Gol'—how can you talk like that?

BENNY

Oh—don't be too cherry, hey. If it bothers you so much, you shouldn't have taken the job. Thinking about it, this is the only job you could do.

SKIN

That's not funny, Benny. Hey, Benny? When are they supposed to—you know, pick him up?

BENNY

The sheriff said early tonight. He has to drive all the way to Oswego, and then turn around, and then he'll be here.

SKIN

So, what? About an hour?

BENNY

Yeah, but don't worry. I'll tell you when it's time, Skin. We'll get more money the longer he takes. All we have to do is watch him, and then help load him up into the hearse.

SKIN

God—I wish he'd hurry. I wish I would have brought some chips with me.

BENNY

Here, eat this.

SKIN

That's not funny, Benny. We just barely aired it out. God. Why're you always picking on me? I ain't done nothing to you.

BENNY

See, when they sent you to that school, they went and made you soft. Christ. Can't even tease you anymore.

SKIN

You're just mean, is all. I hope that sheriff guy comes—soon.

BENNY

Why? You scared? Didn't think you were that smart to be afraid.

SKIN

No, I ain't scared. And I know lots of stuff.

BENNY

Don't lie. You're scared, you soft-headed mutt. I bet you are.

SKIN

No I'm not. I just never did anything like this.

BENNY

Easier then bucking bales.

SKIN

Why are we even here?

BENNY

Well, if Clarence here was murdered, they want to make sure no one touches the body. Remember Sam Rider? They didn't have a place to put him, waiting for the hearse to come. They put his body in a shack like this, and a dog got at him.

SKIN

Jesus.

BENNY

And then some more dogs came. It was difficult when it came time to examine his body. Poor guy. I sure in the hell would hate to have that happen to me.

SKIN

Me, too. Is that what they think, or did he just pass out and freeze?

BENNY

I don't know. Murder maybe? That's what I heard. Clarence over there, just got his oil-lease money and was leaving the bar. They found him by the grain elevator the next day. No money, just a half-empty bottle of muscatel. Hey! Weren't you and Johnny Smokes drinking with him that night?

SKIN

We didn't do anything!

BENNY

Don't get jumpy. I was just asking if you two guys were drinking with him that night.

SKIN

Yeah. Well, he's my uncle. He saw me and bought me a few drinks. I couldn't stay, because I'm staying at my aunt Myrtle's house and I had to be in by a certain time or she'd lock me out.

BENNY

She still has her grandkids with her?

SKIN

Yeah, but when I left, Uncle Clarence was having a good time. Betty French was snuggling up to him.

BENNY

Maybe it was her, huh? Wanting all his money.

SKIN

No. Betty wouldn't do that.

BENNY

What would you know about women. Jesus. Hey, you never know. She rolled ol' Kevin Lincoln for his soc. check one time. Hey! Put more wood in that stove. Don't be expecting me to do everything!

SKIN

It wasn't Betty.

BENNY

How come you call him "Uncle"? You're not even related to him.

SKIN

Yes I am. My mom was his second cousin. She was from the Lambert's on Fort Belknap. And his sister, Eva, was from Fort Belknap.

BENNY

Oh yeah, I forgot about that.

SKIN

You know, he looks different somehows.

BENNY

He's dead. What is he supposed to look like?

SKIN

That isn't what I mean. You know what I mean.

BENNY

You've never seen a dead man before?

SKIN

No. I mean, he was always smiling.

BENNY

He's doing that now.

SKIN

But—but it's different.

BENNY

It should be different—he was alive then, and now he's dead.

SKIN

You know what I mean!

BENNY

No, I don't. What are you working up on? Are you going to cry? Huh? Skin? Are you going to cry?

SKIN

What if I do? None of your business anyways. He was my uncle, you know.

BENNY

You shouldn't have taken this job, then. Christ.

SKIN

Well, it was offered to me. They asked me.

BENNY

No. Usually, me and Tiny Rose do it. You? They found you at the post office and they just asked you because you look hard up. Christ. Tiny is a hell of a lot funner than you.

SKIN

You going to the wake?

BENNY

Of course.

SKIN

The funeral, too?

BENNY

Gosh, I don't know. I'll have to check my appointment book. Gee, Skin, you're not that ringy. I probably will be. There isn't much else to do in this town.

SKIN

God—why do you always think like that, Benny?

BENNY

Like what?

SKIN

People are always talking about how mean you are. They say, "Benny Horses is a mean man. You watch out for him, Skin."

BENNY

They baby you, is all. Anyways, it isn't being mean, it's the truth.

SKIN

Oh. We're related. That makes him your relation, too.

BENNY

Only by marriage. My wife gets mad when I say that, but it's the truth.

SKIN

Gee, he was a full blood, too. The rolls are getting smaller now, enit?

BENNY

More money for me the next per cap, aye.

SKIN

Jesus, Benny. You—you're not that bad, are you?

BENNY

Yeah. Why should I care? You think the sheriff really cares that Clarence is dead? Hell. It's just another Indin killing another Indin is all. Put more wood on that fire.

SKIN

Hey! Listen? Did you hear that?

BENNY

What? Did he fart again? Goddamn it, Clarence.

SKIN

No. It wasn't that.

BENNY

What? Did you fart again?

SKIN

No! It sounded like someone singing.

BENNY

Christ. You're losing it, Skin. Just throw another piece of wood on the fire. You're just spooked, is all. Ever since they found you with Joe-Joe Beans, you've been acting spooky as all hell.

SKIN

No. That ain't true. Anyways, what do you know about that?

BENNY

Hell, who doesn't. You were sixteen and you two guys went out hunting. You guys crossed over the reservation and was poaching on the Z-bar ranch. Joe-Joe was shot by that rancher, enit?

SKIN

I don't know. I didn't see it. All I saw was Joe-Joe go down. I ran over to him and drug him down that hill. I thought he was still, you know, alive.

BENNY

And you were with him until the next day hiding in some brush, enit?

SKIN

Yeah. Wait. It wasn't that bad.

BENNY

If you were sober that day, maybe you would've saw what happened.

SKIN

To hell with you, hey! I wasn't drunk.

BENNY

That's what the county sheriff's deputy told the BIA cops. And that's what everyone else was saying. You were bad, Skin.

SKIN

Well, they're wrong. It didn't happen that way. Joe-Joe was the one who wanted to cross over, not me.

BENNY

But you went anyway.

SKIN

I don't wanna talk about it anymore.

BENNY

Must be true then, huh?

SKIN

Just shut up then, Benny.

BENNY

Hey, Skin? I believe you. No—really. I do.

SKIN

Leave me alone.

BENNY

No. I do. Most guys would've cut out of there, but you did try and stay with Joe-Joe. Well, that's what I think. Damn. It must be thirty below out there. Cold, enit?

SKIN

What are you doing?

BENNY

Nothing. Just look at him.

SKIN

Well, get away from him. We're not supposed to touch him. The sheriff guy said . . .

BENNY

Who's touching? I'm just looking at him.

SKIN

Really?

BENNY

Yeah. Come here, Skin. Look. You know what? He does look different.

SKIN

You think so? Me, too. I think he looks—kinda different.

BENNY

Yeah.

SKIN

Did you hear that?

BENNY

No.

SKIN

That almost sounded like a voice.

BENNY

Oh, come on. Sounded like a voice? I suppose. God, you're jumpy.

SKIN

No, really, Benny. It did.

BENNY

Behave. Hey, look. What is that?

SKIN

What? Oh, that. That's one of his medals he won during the Korean War.

BENNY

Why did he wear it?

SKIN

Don't know. He said it was a reminder.

BENNY

A lot of Indins around here have those. A lot of these boys went off to fight. Came back and there wasn't anything for them. Just like their grandfathers. Didn't mean anything then, doesn't mean anything today.

SKIN

What do you mean?

BENNY

Well, the sheriff won't care who he arrests, just as long as he arrests someone for this. To them, we're one in the same, makes no difference.

SKIN

Yeah, but he's different. Veteran and all.

BENNY

Doesn't matter. I bet they don't even mention it in the newspaper.

SKIN

Okay, I'll bet you.

BENNY

But you have to pay. And I mean real money. Not those damn bottle tops.

SKIN

Yeah. All right.

BENNY

I won this already. I checked the newspaper today, and it should have been in there, and it wasn't. Didn't mention his name at all.

SKIN

Wait—the next newspaper comes out next Monday. Check that one.

BENNY

I will, but he won't be in there. They'll just say some Indin was found near the elevators and the police are looking for someone—that's it.

SKIN

Really? Huh.

BENNY

Yep. Cause I know. We don't mean anything to these white people. Hey, he still kept his teeth, though. Look.

SKIN

Ah-ver! Get away from there, Benny.

BENNY

Skin, remember? He's dead. He doesn't mind—hell, he doesn't even know.

SKIN

If you don't knock it off, I'm gonna do something.

BENNY

No, no, Skin. Look—if you move his lips this way, what does he look like to you?

SKIN

Knock it off, Benny!

BENNY

Kinda reminds me of a carp, enit?

SKIN

Don't, Benny! I'll get mad!

BENNY

Oh, Christ. I'm just having a little fun. Look—you push down his nose, he looks like one of them Hollywood movie Indins.

SKIN

I'm gonna tell, Benny.

BENNY

You know what? We should see what else he has on him, besides those old medals.

Benny begins to go through Clarence's pockets. The door of the shack bursts open. A loud, shrill sound fills the room and the door slams shut. Clarence slowly rises into a sitting position. Benny is horrified and makes a run for the door, colliding with the wood stove and knocking it down. He gets to his feet and runs screaming out the door. Skin stands still and then slowly approaches Clarence.

SKIN

Uncle Clarence?

Blackout.

Rez Politics

A SHORT PLAY IN ONE ACT

Characters

CURTIS: a large boy about ten

GERALD: smaller in size, about ten

PLACE: A field in Montana.

TIME: Early 1970s, afternoon.

Two kids stand in a field of yellow weeds, staring at each other. The ground is gray and dusty from a lack of water. Curtis, one of the kids, is wearing a T-shirt and has his fist clenched. The other boy, Gerald, wears Levis and has on a shirt. They both drop small rocks from their hands.

CURTIS

My dad says you guys are nothing but a bunch of niggers.

GERALD

Yeah? But you guys aren't even Indian. You guys aren't even from here.

CURTIS

Yeah? So?

GERALD

Doesn't make you better than us.

CURTIS

Shit. You and your whole family are nothing but breeds.

GERALD

You too.

CURTIS

But we're more Indian than you guys.

GERALD

No you're not.

CURTIS

That's what my family said.

GERALD

They're wrong, too.

CURTIS

So—you want to fight?

GERALD

I don't know.

CURTIS

Bet you can't fight.

GERALD

I'm not afraid of you.

CURTIS

I bet you are. Damn nigger.

GERALD

To hell with you, Curtis. I thought we were supposed to be friends.

CURTIS

I guess you thought wrong.

GERALD

Why are you doing this, anyway? I didn't do anything to you.

CURTIS

Yes you did.

GERALD

What then?

CURTIS

You know.

GERALD

No I don't.

CURTIS

You're just trying to get out of this. You know what you did. Lying nigger.

Curtis, the larger of the two boys, takes a swing and hits Gerald, knocking him to the ground. Gerald stays on the ground.

GERALD

Fucker! Ow! You fucker!

CURTIS

Get up, Gerald. Get up!

GERALD

Why did you hit me, you fucker?

CURTIS

Get up!

Gerald slowly rubs his face and gets to his feet. Curtis slowly starts to prance. He is ready to fight as Gerald begins to circle.

GERALD

You shit!

CURTIS

Come on. What are you going to do about it? Cry? Come on, Gerald, let's fight.

GERALD

All right, you ass!

Curtis moves in to strike again, but Gerald steps out of the way. Curtis draws back again to swing and this time is caught off guard by Gerald's speed. Gerald strikes Curtis in the stomach, and as Curtis falls forward, Gerald hits him in the face.

CURTIS

You fucker! Ow! Ow!

GERALD

You want to fight? Huh? Huh? Still want to fight?

Gerald plants his foot into Curtis's side.

You fucking breed!

CURTIS

Stop! I didn't hit you when you were down.

GERALD

Well, I'm not down.

CURTIS

Quit it!

GERALD

Are you going to cry? Huh?

CURTIS

Knock it off, you fucking nigger!

GERALD

Stop calling me that!

Kicks Curtis again.

CURTIS

Indins aren't supposed to be fighting each other.

GERALD

Oh—I'm an Indin now, huh?

CURTIS

I didn't say you weren't an Indian.

GERALD

Then why did you try to fight me then, huh?

CURTIS

Because—because I was told to.

GERALD

Who—who told you to fight me?

CURTIS

My brother, Gary. He told me I should kick your black ass.

GERALD

Piss on you, Curtis.

Gerald hits Curtis.

CURTIS

Ow! Stop it! Let me get up. You couldn't do this, if I could get up.

GERALD

No, you stay there. I won't let you up until you tell me why your brother Gary wants you to beat me up.

CURTIS

I already told you. He doesn't like you, your brother, or your sisters because you guys are all part colored.

GERALD

Well, I play around with you, and you're part white.

CURTIS

That isn't the same.

GERALD

Why?

CURTIS

We're part Indian and white.

GERALD

So?

CURTIS

You're part colored.

GERALD

Yeah, but you guys aren't full bloods either.

CURTIS

I know.

GERALD

So why's Gary mad at me?

CURTIS

Because you guys are part black.

GERALD

I didn't do anything to you.

CURTIS

I know.

GERALD

Gee, Curtis. I thought we were friends.

CURTIS

We were, I guess.

GERALD

If your brother doesn't like me so much, why didn't he try to fight me after school today?

CURTIS

Because he's afraid of your older brother, Lewis.

GERALD

I should go and tell Lewis.

CURTIS

No! If you do, Lewis will beat up Gary, and then when Gary finds out, he'll beat me up.

GERALD

Why shouldn't I? We aren't friends.

CURTIS

Let me up—please, Gerald?

GERALD

Okay.

Allows Curtis to get to his feet.

If you try anything, I'll beat you up again.

CURTIS

I won't do anything.

GERALD

All right.

CURTIS

Gerald, I—I didn't mean any of this.

GERALD

What do you mean?

CURTIS

I wasn't going to hurt you.

GERALD

Then why did you try to fight me?

CURTIS

I don't know.

GERALD

Gee, Curtis. Remember when Kenneth and his friends caught you by the water fountain yesterday and starting hitting you? I was the one who stuck up for you.

CURTIS

Yeah, I remember.

GERALD

They were beating you up because you were a breed.

CURTIS

Yeah, I know.

GERALD

So why are you making fun of me and my family?

CURTIS

I don't know, Gerald. I guess I already told you.

GERALD

Yeah, but why?

CURTIS

I don't know. Maybe it's because my dad calls your dad "nigger" all the time.

GERALD

What?

CURTIS

Yeah. Whenever your dad comes over and when he leaves, my dad always says, "I'm glad that damn nigger Stan left."

GERALD

Really?

CURTIS

Yeah. And then he says,"We might not be full blooded, but at least we ain't part niggers like those Robes."

GERALD

Your dad says that?

CURTIS

All the time. What's wrong?

GERALD

We're not part nigger.

CURTIS

Yes you guys are.

GERALD

How would you know?

CURTIS

When Lewis used to grow his hair long, it was always curly. That's how everyone knows.

GERALD

Yeah, but your dad is bald.

CURTIS

That's because we're part white.

GERALD

And you guys aren't even from here.

CURTIS

What do you mean?

GERALD

We're Assiniboines. We're from here. You guys are Crees from South Dakota.

CURTIS

Yeah, but we're Indins.

GERALD

But not from here.

CURTIS

Yeah, but still we're not—well, you know.

GERALD

Do you believe what your dad says?

CURTIS

Yeah. I guess I do. Sort of.

GERALD

I guess we shouldn't be around each other, huh?

CURTIS

I don't know.

GERALD

Should I come over to your house and get my bat?

CURTIS

I don't know.

GERALD

And you should come over and get your BB rifle.

CURTIS

And my army men?

GERALD

No. We left them at your house yesterday when we were playing at the hill.

CURTIS

Gerald? Are you mad?

GERALD

About what?

CURTIS

You know, what I did?

GERALD

I don't know. I'm mad at you, Gary, and your dad.

CURTIS

My father probably didn't mean it. He drinks a lot.

GERALD

Yeah, but what about Gary?

CURTIS

I wouldn't worry about him. I don't even like him. He's always hitting me.

GERALD

Yeah. Like that last time we stole his lighter to pop our firecrackers. He really got mad.

CURTIS

Yeah. Stupid shit.

They laugh.

GERALD

Did your dad ever give his lighter back to him?

CURTIS

No. He still has it.

Pause.

Gerald? Do you—you know, get mad when other kids call you nigger? I know I would.

GERALD

Yeah, I do. I don't like it.

CURTIS

How did you—how did you guys get to be that way, you know?

GERALD

I don't know. I never asked my mom or my dad. How did you guys get to be part white?

CURTIS

My mom says it's because my dad is part white. What about you?

GERALD

I don't know.

CURTIS

Well, didn't your mom tell you it was because of your dad?

GERALD

No. My mom and dad never talk about things like that. At least I've never heard them. They're always laughing and teasing. I remember one time my dad came home really mad one time.

CURTIS

Yeah? Why?

GERALD

This was about a few months ago. He and Lewis went out to get some wood last Saturday to sell. And you know the Krantzes?

CURTIS

You mean David Krantz's family?

GERALD

Yeah. They told my dad they would buy wood from him. Then when my dad and Lewis got back, Krantz wouldn't pay for it. My dad asked him why, but Krantz said my dad was trying to steal from him and there would be no way in hell he would buy wood from a nigger.

CURTIS

Really? After he said he would?

GERALD

Yeah. My dad came into the house and slammed the door. All of us kids went running into the back room. But I stayed. I never did see him that way before.

CURTIS

What happened? Did he hit your mom?

GERALD

No.

CURTIS

My dad is always hitting my mom. We don't eat on time, she spills something, no money when he wants to buy beer—hits her all the time.

GERALD

No, my dad has never done anything like that. He just gets mad and walks away. But this time, he looked different. My mom walked over to him and tried to hug him, I guess, and then with just one arm, he threw off her arms. It was pretty scary. Her arms just went flying. I thought he was going to hit her.

CURTIS

Did he?

GERALD

Huh-uh.

CURTIS

I bet he would've. My dad used to make sure we weren't around—now he don't even care.

GERALD

No, my dad didn't hit my mom. He grabbed her. Hugged her. Like this.

CURTIS

Hey. Don't do that.

GERALD

Well, you asked.

CURTIS

Don't do that.

GERALD

Then, I don't know. I'm not too sure.

CURTIS

What?

GERALD

I think he started to cry.

CURTIS

Wow! Really?

GERALD

I don't know. I was hiding and could barely see them. And I could barely hear him when he talked.

CURTIS

What was he saying?

GERALD

Something about going back to Krantz and hitting him.

CURTIS

Really? Did he do it?

GERALD

No—at least I don't think so. All I remember was my mom saying, "I married an Indian man. I married an Indian man."

CURTIS

Was she crying, too?

GERALD

No. She was just hugging my dad. He tried to pull her off, but he couldn't.

CURTIS

Well, my dad would've. Would've sent my mom flying across the room.

GERALD

No, my dad wouldn't do that—I think.

CURTIS

Did your dad go over to Krantzes?

GERALD

No. They just stood there for a few minutes. Then she let him go and she made him something to eat.

CURTIS

Oh.

GERALD

Well, you want to go over to your house so I can get my bat?

CURTIS

Yeah. I guess.

GERALD

What's wrong?

CURTIS

I just wanted to hold on to it a couple of more days.

GERALD

Why?

CURTIS

You know, to play with it and stuff.

GERALD

But we can't. If I come over now, Gary might not be home, I won't get beat up.

CURTIS

Yeah.

GERALD

Wait. You can keep it.

CURTIS

Yeah, but I want my BB gun back.

GERALD

Yeah. You can come over and get it.

CURTIS

Maybe I can get it tomorrow.

GERALD

You sure?

CURTIS

What do you want to do?

GERALD

I don't know.

CURTIS

I think—yeah, I should go home. My dad should be back by now.

GERALD

Are you going to tell?

CURTIS

What?

GERALD

Are you going to tell him about our fight?

CURTIS

No.

GERALD

What about Gary?

CURTIS

No. He'll get mad because I couldn't beat you up. He'll make fun of me and tell me I couldn't beat up a nigger.

GERALD

Yeah. I'll see you, Curtis.

CURTIS

Maybe we can play tomorrow.

GERALD

I don't know, Curtis. We should wait and see.

CURTIS

Yeah, I guess you're right. Okay. I'll see you then, tomorrow.

GERALD

Yeah. Maybe.

CURTIS

Are you going to tell Lewis?

GERALD

Yeah.

CURTIS

Why?

GERALD

Because you tried to beat me up.

CURTIS

Do you think he'll beat me up?

GERALD

No.

CURTIS

What about Gary?

GERALD

Yeah.

CURTIS

Then don't tell him, Gerald. Cause if you do, I'll get it.

GERALD

Are you crying?

CURTIS

Yeah. Because I don't want Gary to beat me up!

GERALD

Okay, Curtis, okay. I won't.

CURTIS

Promise?

GERALD

Yeah, I promise.

CURTIS

I won't listen to that dumb shit Gary again.

GERALD

Yeah, I guess you shouldn't.

CURTIS

You know what, Gerald?

GERALD

What?

CURTIS

I like you. You know why?

GERALD

No. Why?

CURTIS

Because my dad is always saying stuff about how you can't trust niggers. I trust you, Gerald.

GERALD

That's because I'm not a nigger, Curtis. I'm an Indian.

CURTIS

Yeah. Right. We're Indians. I guess we shouldn't have even been fighting, huh?

GERALD

Yeah. I guess we shouldn't be fighting.

CURTIS

Well, I'm going to go home, Gerald. See you tomorrow.

GERALD

Yeah. Bye, Curtis.

Curtis begins to exit.

CURTIS

And you promise you won't tell Lewis?

GERALD

Yeah! I won't! Bye.

Curtis exits. Gerald stand still for a moment. A second rock from his fist falls to the ground. He begins to shake violently. Blackout.

The Council

A PLAY IN ONE ACT

Characters

BEING ONE: Joey, Man

BEING TWO: Whale One, Condor, Ice Traveler (Orca Whale), Woman

BEING THREE: Scientist, Sparrow, Walrus, Man Three, Wolf One.

BEING FOUR: Whale Two, Tiger, Sea Turtle, Woman Two, Wolf Two.

BEING FIVE: Father, Panda Bear, Man One.

BEING SIX: Whale Three, Sea Gull, Lizard, Man Two.

BEING SEVEN: Michelle, Eagle, Wolf, Mako, Water Buffalo Calf, Woman One.

PROLOGUE

There are three banners in the air. They are whales. One by one the whales beach themselves on the ground. A father and his two children, Michelle and Joey, enter.

MICHELLE

Oh Daddy, look.

JOEY

What are they, Daddy?

FATHER

Whales. They must have beached themselves a few minutes ago.

MICHELLE

Are they still alive? Hey, Daddy. Look at those men over there, Daddy. Maybe they'll know what to do—you think so?

FATHER

Yes, maybe. Michelle and Joey, you stay here and don't touch anything. I'm going over to ask one of those men if they know what's going on. I'll be right back.

He begins to exit, and Joey follows him. Father stops and takes Joey back to Michelle.

I said I'll be right back.

Father exits. Then one of the whales makes a sound.

MICHELLE

Do you hear that, Joey? It sounds like one of them's trying to say something.

JOEY

No they're not. You're just trying to scare me.

MICHELLE

Don't be such a geek. I am not—just listen.

WHALE ONE

A long time ago,

WHALES TOGETHER

Grandchildren,

WHALE ONE

The world was young and new. Always changing. The changes of

WHALES TOGETHER

fire, floods, earthquakes, tornadoes, hurricanes,

WHALE ONE

made the first beings join together for their own survival. It was then they decided they would have

WHALES TOGETHER

Council.

Music as actors freeze on stage. Blackout.

SCENE ONE

Man is on stage. He is trying to fly by flapping his arms. Sea Gull, Eagle, Sparrow, and then Condor enter. Sea Gull pokes Man and causes a stir. They settle down to a quiet state.

SEA GULL

He won't, he can't, he can't fly. What a goofy being.

EAGLE

Quiet, Sea Gull.

SPARROW

There is a possibility he will go to the Council.

MAN

What's this "Council" thing, anyway. I don't want to go. I want to stay with my own nation.

CONDOR

No. We were told to bring you to the Council, Man. You have to appear before the Council. Now, climb on my back and I'll take you there.

SEA GULL

A long, a long way, a long journey to have.

MAN

From here to the Council?

SEA GULL

No, no—I mean, from Condor's back, when in the sky, to the ground is a long way to splat.

CONDOR

Don't say things like that to him. Eagle, Sparrow, help him get on my back.

EAGLE

Man, be brave. Do it now. Condor is the strongest of all of us, and she'll take you there safely.

MAN

All right. Maybe one of these days I'll make the journey myself.

Birds laugh.

SEA GULL

Don't, don't, don't fa . . . don't splat.

MAN

Thanks a lot.

The birds begin to take off. Condor is the last to take off.

EAGLE

Farewell, Man.

SPARROW

Bye, oh—bye, bye, bye.

Condor and Man are in the air.

MAN

I want—I want to fly by myself!

CONDOR

You're not made for it.

MAN

What do you mean?

CONDOR

I have feathers and the ability to fly.

MAN

If I had feathers, could I fly?

CONDOR

I don't know.

Man examines the feathers on Condor's back. He begins to pick one.

Some of our relations have feathers and can't fly. Ow. There are some of them who are very fast runners and can't fly. Ow. What are you doing, Man?

MAN

Just borrowing some feathers.

Man has picked several feathers, and Condor is having problems flying.

CONDOR

What? Ow! Why?

MAN

So I can fly by myself.

CONDOR

Man! No! You can't fly! And I can't fly if you take my feathers.

MAN

Yes, I can.

Man takes the feathers he has plucked from Condor, jumps off of Condor's back, and tries to flap his arms.

I can, I can go . . . I'm gonna go "splat"!

He comes crashing to the ground. The Council gathers around him. (Condor, Wolf, Tiger, Panda Bear, Walrus, and Lizard)

TIGER

Members of the council, I give you our new being, "Man."

Wolf walks over and sniffs Man.

WOLF

So this is how it looks up close. It's still alive.

Man stirs, and Wolf brushes dirt on him and walks away.

WALRUS

Oh, bother. I was hoping this wouldn't take so long.

CONDOR

As a representative of my nation and all my relations, I thank you for the chance to bring this new being to the Council. If you don't need me for anything else, I would like to return to my home.

TIGER

Yes—thank you, Condor. You are excused.

Condor exits.

LIZARD

What (*Pause*) shall we do with this silly being?

TIGER

Lizard, my old friend, that's why we are here. All of you, Talkers from the nations and your relations, what are we to do with this new being, "Man"?

WOLF

I, Wolf, say we should get rid of him and his small herd.

TIGER

Then I take it we're in agreement not to let this being live with us?

PANDA BEAR

Excuse me, Tiger and other distinguished Talkers of the Council, but we can't do that. If a cloud passes into the empty sky, we can't prevent it from doing so. He comes from the earth just as we do.

WALRUS

Perhaps he will go away. Pass on. Remember, Panda Bear, remember Lizard's nations and all their relations had beings that passed on. Some of his relations had wings and flew in the sky, and they had no feathers. The ancient ones. They passed away—frightening beings they were.

WOLF

You may be right, Walrus. Man and his nations may not survive if they don't learn to feed themselves. Man's nation has been taking the remains from our hunts, but they need to learn to hunt for themselves.

TIGER

If a claw poked its skin, the skin would open. Its skin feels so thin.

WALRUS

Look! Not only is it thin skinned, but it grows plants on itself.

PANDA BEAR

Walrus, my large friend, these plants aren't growing from it. Man takes these plants to cover himself.

WOLF

Should we allow it to pass away or live amongst us?

PANDA BEAR

The Council and all the nations would have to make an exception. We should not hunt them until they've become larger in numbers and stronger in health.

TIGER

No. Full members of the Council hunt and are hunted. It's the circle of life . . .

LIZARD

They are weak of body. They could be weak of mind. If this is so, they will never learn our ways.

PANDA BEAR

We teach our cubs who are weak and don't know the ways. We can teach it the same things. Man will learn, but we have to protect this new being until it has developed its own skills and builds its strength . . .

WALRUS

Protect it? See here, Panda Bear. No one protects our young for us.

PANDA BEAR

Call for a vote.

There is no other way for them to survive. Agree?

WALRUS

Oh all right, Panda Bear.

Vote is taken and won.

They will not be hunted.

WOLF

Will it be a Talker for itself, or should we chose a Talker for it since it is so weak?

PANDA BEAR

Wolf, it has to be able to talk for itself. It has a mouth, I think.

Panda Bear examines Man.

WALRUS

Because he and his nation are so young, he should have a Talker who is already recognized and established in bloodlines to talk for him and his nation.

PANDA BEAR

Who is the closest relation to Man? Doesn't anyone want to claim relationship to the new being?

Whale sound.

ICE TRAVELER

Me, me—I will.

Council members stir.

PANDA BEAR

Now, this is very interesting. Someone wants to serve as a Talker for Man. Here is Ice Traveler of the Orca nations and all their relations.

WALRUS

Ice Traveler? Oh dear. I'd rather be splatted, myself.

WOLF

Really? Who could lift you?

TIGER

Silence! We will meet with Ice Traveler.

Council members cross to the edge of the stage. Ice Traveler is represented by a banner. He comes to a stop and the Council members gather near him. Man lies motionless on the stage.

ICE TRAVELER

Members of the Council, I will see to it that Man and his nations grow strong. They will become a proud nation of the Council. We are all different, but we must live together as one, and he will be taught this. I will ask help from other Council members to teach Man and his nations to live.

Panda Bear steps forward.

WOLF

You and Panda Bear will make sure he understands and learns the Council's ways, Ice Traveler?

ICE TRAVELER

Yes, I will. We will all teach them.

LIZARD

Silliness!

ICE TRAVELER

If I am wrong, then he will pass away like other nations of the past.

Man stirs, and Council members cross to him.

MAN

I, me, I—I splatted. Ow! My arm is sore, too.

Panda Bear is face to face with Man.

What? I, I—I mean, who are you?

PANDA BEAR

Panda Bear, Talker of the Panda Bear nation and all their relations.

MAN

The Council. I made it? I didn't think I would get here.

PANDA BEAR

Yes. Would you like to wrestle? Best two out of three?

MAN

No, no—thank you, but nah. Uh—am I and my people to be included in the Council? We can use more help. Wolf and his nations have been helpful in providing food, but we don't get enough to eat. We are the fourth ones to eat after Wolf and the other nations.

PANDA BEAR

Man, you'll be heard and fed. Things will change for you and your people. Your markings will soon join ours in the Council circle.

Man walks around the circle. He is about to place his hand print.

Wait,—you'll have to wait.

MAN

Uh—I thank you, all of you. I'm, uh—I'm going to get something to sit on.

Man exits off stage. The Council members re-form into Council stances in circle.

TIGER

Members of the Council, when Man has grown, we will allow him to place his markings at the edge of the Council circle with ours. Then he will become the Talker of his nation and join the circle of life.

Man enters with a small hide. This causes a large uproar among the Council members until Tiger restores order.

WOLF

Look!

TIGER

What is that?

PANDA BEAR

Answer, Man.

MAN

I needed something to sit on. The idea came to me, so I'm going to use this mangy old hide.

TIGER

Where did you get—get this "hide"?

MAN

From over there. There were a lot of them.

WALRUS

That hide is from the resting place of the Council members we honor.

COUNCIL MEMBERS

Man! Silliness! Silly thing! Strange Being! Greedy pup!

Blackout.

SCENE TWO

Tiger is hiding in some bushes. Man and Panda Bear enter. When they do, Tiger stalks them.

PANDA BEAR

You are fortunate that no being is allowed to be attacked or hunted at a Council. Be sure to think before you take.

Tiger charges out and knocks Man down.

TIGER

What—what a strange cub. So skinny.

PANDA BEAR

Now, first we are going to have Tiger teach you how to hunt. That will be your first path to learning the ways of this world. Kill only to hunt and to protect.

MAN

Hunt? Oh, you mean to get food?

TIGER

You have to eat, don't you? Where is your partner?

MAN

Don't have one. Why should I have one?

TIGER

No wonder you're starving.

PANDA BEAR

First you must know what fills your stomach.

MAN

You mean, what is it we eat?

TIGER

Yes.

MAN

Do you have any grubs in this land?

TIGER

Grubs? You'll feed a whole family and a nation on grubs?

MAN

Everything else is too fast or too big for us to hunt.

TIGER

Then I will show you how to hunt those who are too fast and too big for you to catch.

MAN

All right. "Hear me, O too big and too fast" . . .

TIGER

Silence! Silence! Now, there is a water buffalo calf over there.

MAN

Really? Where?

TIGER

Smell it.

MAN

I can't smell it. Are you sure . . .

TIGER

Will you be silent! Shhh—it's coming this way.

MAN

What are you going to do when it gets here?

TIGER

I will surprise it and jump on it. I'll go for its neck and then bring it down—humph! And what will you do, Man?

MAN

Oh—run like a four legged ostrich in the other direction.

TIGER

No, no. You will come from the other side. Now watch closely. Soon it will come out of the weeds, and you'll have something for your family to eat.

She exits into the bushes. Man doesn't. Tiger chases Man to Panda Bear, who is hiding in the bushes. She returns to bushes.

MAN

Panda Bear, I don't know if I can do it.

PANDA BEAR

Shhh—trust her, Man. She is a great hunter for her nation.

MAN

Yeah, but she has things. She has claws, teeth, and a lot of other things I don't have.

PANDA BEAR

You have claws.

Examines Man's hands.

Or the beginnings of claws. You have teeth.

MAN

But I can't do what she does. I need something else.

He begins to look around in the bushes. He finds a stick and a rock, then a vine.

PANDA BEAR

Now what are you doing, Man? Man?

Man places the rock on the stick and uses the vine to wrap the rock to the stick.

MAN

Making a claw.

From another part of the stage, Water Buffalo Calf enters. Tiger takes a final sniff.

WATER BUFFALO CALF

Ma? Ma? Ma? Ma? Ma?

Tiger stalks toward Water Buffalo Calf, but before she can attack, Man has also charged and strikes Tiger with claw and then gives a loud charging cry and chases Water Buffalo Calf offstage. Panda Bear and Tiger freeze, watching him, then look at each other.

TIGER

He can't be taught anything.

PANDA BEAR

He was only trying to help you.

TIGER

Now what do I feed my family?

PANDA BEAR

He didn't mean to ruin your hunt. I'm sure he'll take responsibility for what he's done.

TIGER

I should feed him to my family.

PANDA BEAR

Remember our agreement. Man is not to be hunted.

TIGER

Then you teach him how to hunt.

She exits. Man enters with a melon.

MAN

Look—look what I knocked out of a tree with my claw.

Proudly displays club.

Now I have to work on making myself some teeth. Where's Tiger?

PANDA BEAR

She's not—not too pleased at this moment.

MAN

It wasn't my fault. She got in my way.

PANDA BEAR

Oh, Man. You have a lot to learn about the hunt. I still think you should learn to, to—to wrestle.

He playfully charges Man. Man doesn't know what to do, but he raises the club in defense. Panda Bear senses the pose and withdraws. Man drops the melon and club and runs to Panda Bear. They embrace. Panda Bear laughs.

SCENE THREE

Ice Traveler and Sea Turtle are on stage. Ice Traveler is in the water and Sea Turtle is on the beach.

SEA TURTLE

Lizard didn't agree with my helping you, Ice Traveler, but you—I like you. Just call me.

ICE TRAVELER

Like this?

Whale sound.

SEA TURTLE

Beautiful.

ICE TRAVELER

Thank you, Sea Turtle. Man must learn about other nations and where they live.

Man enters, carrying a lance.

MAN

Hello, Ice Traveler, and—and, whatever you, uh—hi.

ICE TRAVELER

Hello. This is my friend, Sea Turtle. Today we have another kind of world to show you, one called "ocean," which we call home.

SEA TURTLE

I don't wish to sound bothersome, but what is that thing you are carrying?

MAN

It's something new I've made. I have watched other beings hunt with their large teeth. My teeth are small. This will be my tooth—my people call it a "spear"—and now I can take bigger bites.

SEA TURTLE

You still eat? You can bite things?

MAN

But they are little bites.

SEA TURTLE

Then eat only little things.

MAN

I can't survive eating only little things.

SEA TURTLE

Why not? Many of Ice Traveler's relations do.

MAN

Not me.

SEA TURTLE

Why?

MAN

Uh, uh—because!

SEA TURTLE

Oh. I can see a glimmer of understanding there.

ICE TRAVELER

A second way of the Council says, if you go into land marked by another nation, you respect that home and don't leave your markings there.

MAN

This'll be easy. It's only water.

SEA TURTLE

Hmmm, there could be a problem here. The ocean is home to many nations, Man.

ICE TRAVELER

You'll understand it better when you see what we mean, Man. Now, let's start while we still have the sun.

Man tries to get into the water.

SEA TURTLE

Man, you may ride beside me or on my back. Whatever is easier for you.

MAN

Thank you, Sea Turtle.

Man jumps on Sea Turtles back. They go under water, then reappear.

Are we going far?

ICE TRAVELER

Oh yes.

MAN

This water feels funny.

ICE TRAVELER

It is very different from the water you find on land. I'm going ahead of you and Man, Sea Turtle. I want to make sure the path is clear.

Whale sound. Ice Traveler exits.

SEA TURTLE

Don't go too far, Ice Traveler.

Walrus enters. He is fishing.

WALRUS

Hello, Sea Turtle.

SEA TURTLE

Hello, Walrus.

WALRUS

Is that your new offspring? Seems to have lost his shell.

SEA TURTLE

We're busy, Walrus. Man? How do you move in the water?

MAN

I can move fine.

SEA TURTLE

Wonderful, because I'm getting a little weary of carrying you.

Sea Turtle dumps Man into the water. Man panics.

MAN

Help! I'll be—I'll be swallowed. Help me!

SEA TURTLE

Don't be ridiculous. A little water never hurt anyone . . .

WALRUS

Odd being.

MAN

Help!

Swims to Walrus, who splashes him with water.

WALRUS

A bit awkward.

SEA TURTLE

Now, now—remain calm. You'll be all right. Just move your fins, uh—whatever those things are called.

MAN

Hands.

SEA TURTLE

Yes, your fins and hands.

Walrus goes underwater and gets a fish.

WALRUS

Delightful hunting today, don't you think?

Plays with the fish.

MAN

Hey. That's my fish.

SEA TURTLE

We share, Man. There is enough for everyone.

Goes under and gets a fish for Man.

Here.

MAN

But I want that one.

WALRUS

This one? But why?

SEA TURTLE

Yes, why?

MAN

Because, uh—because it's mine!

WALRUS

Oh, very well—here.

Throws fish at Man. It hits him.

MAN

Ow! Hey, you big—you big slug.

Walrus puts fin on top of Man's head and holds him underwater.

WALRUS

Rude little being.

Let's Man up.

Reminds me of the time when I was . . .

Walrus releases Man and sees Mako's fin.

Oh-oh. An unwanted visitor. Shark! Swim everyone. Swim away!

Walrus exits. Mako swims around upstage of Sea Turtle and Man.

MAN

He doesn't frighten me. I have my tooth, you know. No one is going to take my lunch.

SEA TURTLE

Get on my back! We have to flee immediately!

MAN

Sea Turtle, I said I'm not afraid of him.

SEA TURTLE

Oh no! Mako, listen to me! You must not attack us, because—uh, because . . .

MAN

Just because.

SEA TURTLE

No, because we're teaching the new being.

MAKO

Is it tasty? Crunchy, munchy new being. Tasty new being, is it?

MAN

I'm not afraid of him.

Man takes his spear and lunges it forward into Mako's mouth. Mako is hurt, then spits out the spear.

MAKO

It tastes stringy. New being, new being, is that your name? We want to remember you. That way, the next time we meets one of you, we'll know how tasty you all are when we eats you.

MAN

Help!

SEA TURTLE

I thought you said you weren't afraid.

MAN

That was before he took my tooth.

SEA TURTLE/MAN

Help! Ice Traveler! Help!

MAKO

We think we'll have a few fins, tasty, munchy finnies, then the new being. All very tasty and very munchy crunchy.

Mako is ready to make his attack, but Ice Traveler arrives and bumps him. He doesn't see Ice Traveler.

Eee! What is the cause of our hurt? What takes us away from our crunchy munchies?

ICE TRAVELER

These beings are protected by the Council.

MAKO

Council? Yes—we remembers Council. Who cares for the Council? No one tells us whens to eats. We eats whatever is crunchiest and munchiest, babe!

ICE TRAVELER

If you don't leave them alone, I will bump you and bite you.

MAKO

We goes, we goes, nice-eties lady. (*Begins to exit but stops near Man.*) Stay healthies—we don't likes excess fats.

Mako exits.

SEA TURTLE

If you are to fear anything in the world of water, he and all his nations and their relations are the ones to fear, Man. Brutes is what they are.

MAN

The nations should get together and kick them out of the Council.

ICE TRAVELER

No. This is Mako's home, and he belongs here. He has a purpose to the earth as everyone else does. There are good beings like us and then there are those like Mako. They are old members of the Council, but as time went on and they grew in numbers, Mako's brain never changed.

SEA TURTLE

I'm surprised he still remembers the word, "Council."

MAN

Ice Traveler? There are a lot of water beings I haven't met. How do I know which ones to fear and which ones not to?

ICE TRAVELER

Try not to fear other beings, Man. You will know the ones to stay away from and the ones to go to when you're in trouble and need help. Just be watchful.

SEA TURTLE

Here—get on my back. Man—you're heavy. You should eat little things.

Blackout.

SCENE FOUR

Woman is standing near a small blocked stream. She has a spear and is fishing. There are some tall reeds nearby. When she is going to strike, Man enters. He is wearing a headdress made of flowers and weeds. Woman hides behind the reeds and watches.

MAN

I am Man, small water beings. I have come to get you to eat you. Now, do not make me use my tooth. Come out of your homes now!

Woman crosses to Man and thumps him in the rear with her spear.

Ow! Who—who are you?

WOMAN

A being trying to get some food. You scared my food away.

MAN

Not me. I'm getting food for myself.

WOMAN

(*Pointing to headdress*) What' that?

MAN

This? This is to let everyone know that I'm the leader of the nation of Man.

WOMAN

That's very funny. Now, who—what are you?

MAN

Let me introduce myself. Ahem, I am Man. I can talk with all the beings of the Council. Do not fear me, because—I don't fear you. Because I can talk to all the beings of the Council and be heard, I am a leader—a "Talker."

WOMAN

Then go and "talk" somewhere else. I need to eat.

MAN

I—I can help you. I can get food to feed you.

WOMAN

So can I. Man—are you always this noisy when you hunt?

MAN

(*He jumps into stream and fishes.*) No. Just watch. Watch how great—good, I am—was . . .

WOMAN

You'll scare them away.

MAN

Come here, fish beings!

WOMAN

Here. I'll show you how to do it. (*She leads him out of the stream with her spear, then spears a fish.*)

MAN

Uh, that one must have heard me. (*They stand looking at the fish.*) Looks like it's some good food.

WOMAN

Would you like to share my food? I don't think I can eat all of this by myself.

MAN

Sure.

Man removes the fish from the spear and takes a bite out of it.

WOMAN

What are you doing?

MAN

Eating.

WOMAN

The head? Not even prepared! Yuck!

MAN

How else do you eat a water being?

WOMAN

You can eat it raw, but you have to prepare it first. You could season it with some herbs, broast it, roast it, fry it, dry it . . .

MAN

All right. Prepare it. Puh-lease?

WOMAN

Just this once, but you have to clean up after we're done.

They play around and it leads to a kiss. They break off awkwardly.

MAN

Yes, uh—my name is Man. What's yours?

WOMAN

Woman.

MAN

You're nice. Gentle, too.

WOMAN

You're—strange—and gentle, I guess.

She begins to exit. Man follows.

MAN

We can get a lot of things done together, can't we?

WOMAN

After watching you, I don't know.

Man leaves her and jumps back into the stream.

MAN

Hear me, O fish beings. One of you is our meal for today. You should all feel good about that. Next time when I call, I want you all to be ready to . . .

WOMAN

Are you hungry, or do you want to talk?

MAN

I'm hungry, but I want more fish. Not for me, but for us.

WOMAN

We already have a fish for lunch and some other food we can share. Man? If you get more fish . . . Stupid Man!

He doesn't pay attention to her as she exits.

MAN

Come here, O fish beings.

Tries to get one and misses.

If there was only a way of stopping you guys from getting away. Ha!

Takes a stone sitting near the bank and rolls it into the stream. Then finds another stone and does the same.

Now, you have to come to me, O fish beings.

Picks fish out of the water and tosses them onto the bank. Wolf enters and watches him. She slowly sneaks near the fish. Man finally discovers her.

WOLF

Hello, Man. That is a lot of fish you have. I'm hungry. You will not mind if I . . .

MAN

No, Wolf.

WOLF

But Man, we've always shared our food with you.

MAN

After you ate first and took all the good parts.

WOLF

Then I'll wait, like you did.

MAN

No. Get away from me.

Wolf picks up a fish.

Put that down! You can't have any.

Man picks up a rock and throws it.

WOLF

Ow! Man!

Wolf drops the fish. Man gets more rocks to throw.

MAN

Go on.

WOLF

Your supposed to share with—ow—others.

MAN

Leave!

WOLF

Stop it!

Wolf exits. Man slowly gets out of the stream, gathers his fish, and cautiously looks around. He leaves the stream blocked and exits.

SCENE FIVE

Man is kneeling. In front of him is a small pile of twigs. He has two rocks and is rubbing the rocks together. Woman enters. She is listening to the sounds around her. She crosses to Man.

WOMAN

Do you think they will come, Man?

MAN

I don't see why not. Don't be afraid. They are my friends. Why, I'm nearly one of them. When they see this new gift I have for them, they'll be so surprised they'll want to make me a Head Talker.

Wolf enters and howls. Then Panda Bear and Lizard enter. Tiger enters and brushes past Woman.

TIGER

Man, why have you called us to the dens of your nation?

LIZARD

Yes. (*Pause.*) What is wrong? Cannot drink from the stream because it moves too fast for you?

MAN

Wait. You'll see. I have something I want to share with you animals.

PANDA BEAR

We—"animals"? What does "animals" mean?

MAN

I mean, we, "my" nation, are "human beings," and you are just beings—"animals."

PANDA BEAR

Excuse me, but then if we are just beings and you are a being, you are an animal too.

MAN

Okay. I'm a "human animal." Now I have something I want to share with the nations of the Council. It's something I've found. We're using it in our den areas and it's great.

TIGER

We have something to say to you, Man. You must obey the ways . . .

MAN

Yes, yes, yes. Let me show you this first.

Tiger is angered.

PANDA BEAR

Man, please listen to Tiger. We've all come a long way to . . .

MAN

I will, I will. Just wait up.

Tiger rushes Man and knocks him over. This catches everyone off guard.

TIGER

MAN! Man, you and your nation must obey the Council's ways.

MAN

All right, Tiger, all right—but you got to see this first.

He goes back to his rocks and the small pile of twigs. Tiger signals Wolf, and they both start to stalk Man. Just when they are ready to attack, Woman helps Man by striking the rocks together and making a spark for the fire. Man picks up one of the lit pieces of wood.

Behold. I give the nations, uh—"something that's red and hot."

Man drives off Wolf and Tiger.

Don't be afraid of it. It won't bite. Ha!

PANDA BEAR

Excuse me, Man, but we call this "fire."

MAN

"Fire"? You know about this stuff already?

WOLF

We have known about it for many seasons.

Man walks around holding the flaming piece of wood. He chases off Tiger.

MAN

Do you want some fire? What about you?

LIZARD

Excuse me, but get rid of the fire, Man. (*Pause.*) REMOVE IT NOW!

MAN

This is a gift. It's a gift from my nation to the nations of the Council.

Woman crosses to Man and tries to stop him from terrorizing everybody.

I know what I'm doing with it. There's nothing to be afraid of.

WOLF

He grabs ahold of Lizard's tail.

He will hurt all of us. Run. Run!

He drags Lizard offstage. Man follows them.

MAN

No! Stay! It's safe. Panda Bear, Panda Bear—make them stay. It won't hurt them.

Crosses to Panda Bear and prevents him from escaping.

PANDA BEAR

Put it down, Man. Put the fire down.

MAN

All right.

He mindlessly tosses the burning piece of wood. Fire starts. All three turn to look. (The fire can be represented by an actor waving a red banner.)

Oh-oh.

PANDA BEAR

What?

MAN

Run!

Three large banners of red appear onstage and cross and circle the stage area, creating the fire. Wolf enters and dances with the banners. One banner disappears, and she now takes time to catch her breath.)

WOLF

Hurry! Stay with your clan. You will survive this if you stay with your clan.

Wolf fights the banners and Tiger enters challenging the flames.

TIGER

Those of you who can't run, go to the streams and rivers. Hurry! It's getting closer.

She fights off the flames and gets near Wolf.

I want to meet with all the Talkers as soon as we have outdistanced the fire.

Tiger is nearly ready to run when Sparrow flies in and catches her attention.

SPARROW

Tiger, Tiger! I see—I see the fire.

TIGER

How large is it?

SPARROW

It is large, yes—oh, oh, very large.

TIGER

Will we be able to escape it?

SPARROW

Yes, Man helps. Man and his nation help us, we can escape. They are on the other side of the fire.

TIGER

They are safe.

SPARROW

They're tossing dirt and water on the fire—on the fire, oh my.

TIGER

What?

SPARROW

Yes. They're throwing, kicking, splashing dirt and water on the fire—oh yes, yes. We can escape, escape.

Sparrow flies off, and Wolf joins Tiger.

WOLF

Now is the time. We have to do something about Man. This is more of his irresponsibility.

TIGER

Not here. When we meet we'll do something. Now go. Go!

They fight off the flames. The flames change direction, and Man and Woman enter.

MAN

More water! Use the drinking water! Wet the cloth and beat the fire with it.

WOMAN

Man, we can try to change the direction of the fire.

MAN

To the river! Try to lead the fire to the river.

WOMAN

Look at what we've done. All the homes are being destroyed.

MAN

I didn't mean this to happen.

Man and Woman exit. There is one big flash of the red banner. The sounds of the fire fade. Panda Bear, Lizard, Wolf, and Walrus enter. They are all tired and hurt. They try to take care of one another. Tiger enters and examines each Council member.

TIGER

We have time now. I want you, the Talkers, to take back what is decided here and share it with your nation and your relations. Man and his nations have broken the ways. They are now large and strong and grow fat. They are now a full nation. They should be hunted.

PANDA BEAR

This is wrong, Tiger. They aren't strong enough. It's not too late to teach them the ways. We are still responsible for them.

WOLF

Responsible? Man is not responsible.

TIGER

We never know what he will do next. That is the danger.

WALRUS

That's correct. If you've noticed, Man and his nation are now quite large. They have knives, spears, and other things—I don't know what they call them, but they are dangerous to all of us.

LIZARD

They disregard the Council's ways as if the ways don't include them.

TIGER

Something has to be done. My nation and I will not wait for the next danger.

PANDA BEAR

Don't do this, Tiger. Please. We aren't like Mako and his relations. We give the ways time to work. Things will change. They have worked before. I ask all of you to please wait and be patient. Let time show us how things will work out.

TIGER

I say we don't have time. We have to act now.

WALRUS

I agree with Tiger, Panda Bear. We must act now or it'll be too late, and they'll destroy all of us.

PANDA BEAR

I don't believe hunting Man and his nation will solve the problems we face.

TIGER

We don't have time. If we wait, we will pass away, one nation after another.

WALRUS

Then is it settled? Do we agree to allow Man and his nations to be hunted like all the members of the Council?

LIZARD

Yes.

WOLF

Before it becomes too late for all of us.

They call for a vote. Panda Bear withdraws from the vote.

TIGER

Let's begin now.

They vote, then Tiger begins to exit.

PANDA BEAR

Stop, Tiger. I can't allow you to do this.

TIGER

Move out of my path, Panda Bear. It is Man I want.

PANDA BEAR

Then I cannot move. It's wrong, what you are going to do.

TIGER

I hunt to protect. For the survival of my nation.

Tiger stalks and circles Panda Bear. All council members become excited as the possible fight builds.

WALRUS

No. Not at a Council meeting. Stop, both of you!

LIZARD

Young one, don't hinder her. She says it is for protection. That is reason enough.

Tiger and Panda Bear fight, exchanging blows. Wolf helps Tiger by distracting Panda Bear. Tiger charges Panda Bear and knocks him to the ground. She is ready to strike his neck but stops.

TIGER

Hear me! Let your nations know that Man is to be hunted. If anyone in your nations is hurt or killed by Man and his nation, Man will answer to me!

Blackout.

SCENE SIX

Woman is working in a small garden patch. Man sneaks up behind her to surprise her. He does and she reacts by sweeping him off his feet.

WOMAN

Man? Oh, Man. I have something for you to do. Are you all right?

MAN

Don't worry about me. I'm like a rock.

Falls over after she has sat him up.

WOMAN

Good. I want you to help me pull out the weeds so the plants can grow. Do it like this.

Demonstrates how to pull weeds.

Oh—you're going to find these little bugs.

MAN

"Little beings."

WOMAN

Yes. I want you to remove them from the plants. When you finish, we'll eat.

MAN

Will I have to wash my hands before we eat—again?

WOMAN

Yes.

He begins to lick his hands.

Not like that.

MAN

All right.

Woman begins to exit, but stops. She watches Man.

Weeds, weeds—which are the plants and which are the weeds?

Wolf One appears and begins to growl.

WOMAN

Listen. What is that, Man?

Wolf Two appears and growls.

MAN

Hello.

Gets to his feet and walks to the wolves.

What's wrong? Don't you two know who I am?

Woman pulls Man back behind her.

WOMAN

Yes, I believe they don't know who you are.

Wolf Three enters. The Wolves circle Man and Woman, growling.

MAN

Wait a minute. You beings are scouting.

WOMAN

Scouting for what?

MAN

For hunting—wait. Your nation can't hunt us.

Man Two enters, carrying a rock and a spear. He sets his rock down and begins to attack the wolves.

MAN TWO

Get out of here, you bad animals! Get away from here! Go!

Chases them off.

MAN

What are you doing? Come back here.

WOMAN

Were they hunting us? I thought we were not to be hunted.

MAN

Yes. I was told by the Council we would have a chance to grow.

Sea Gull enters.

WOMAN

Do you think they've changed their minds?

Sea Gull crashes into Man and Woman.

SEA GULL

Oh Man, oh Man, oh Man is in for it now.

WOMAN

What's it saying, Man?

SEA GULL

I hate, I wouldn't—I wouldn't want to be in your nest.

MAN

Sea Gull, what are you talking about?

SEA GULL

Good shape, good shape. Need to stay in good shape for the hunt. I don't want to be near you. Might, would, could, mistake me for you. Get away, get away, get lost, Man.

Man Two enters and stalks Sea Gull.

WOMAN

What about the wolves? Ask him if that's what the wolves were doing?

Man Two smacks Sea Gull's bottom with his spear, sending Sea Gull into Man and Woman. Sea Gull bounces off Man and Woman and falls back into a waiting kick by Man Two.

MAN TWO

Get! Get away, you disgusting bird!

Man Two chases Sea Gull.

SEA GULL

Bad, bad, evil Man.

MAN

Sea Gull, wait! You shouldn't have done that. He wasn't bothering anyone.

MAN TWO

Oh—I save both of your lives and that's how you say thanks.

MAN

What's going on?

MAN TWO

We're being attacked! Animals have crashed into the village, biting, scratching, and slashing at everything in sight. It's terrible. At least, that's what I've heard. Move.

MAN

Who told you to do that?

Man Three enters, carrying some spears.

MAN THREE

Get more rocks. Tell the people to get all their knifes, spears, and bows ready. We'll show these animals.

Man Three exits and Man One enters.

MAN

Wait! What's going on?

MAN THREE

What are you two doing standing around? Get busy. We have to defend our villages.

MAN

From what? Ourselves?

MAN THREE

The animals.

Woman Two enters being chased by Tiger.

WOMAN ONE

Help me! Help me!

MAN THREE

Attack the tiger! Drive it back!

Man Three and Man One drive Tiger offstage. Man gets in between them.

MAN

That's a Talker of the Council. Don't hurt her.

WOMAN ONE

Thank you, thank you.

She crosses to Man Three, but he pushes her off to Woman.

MAN THREE

What are you doing? You're sympathizing with the animals! After this poor woman was attacked?

MAN

Yes—I mean, no. Listen. This is getting too crazy. We aren't being attacked. We're being hunted, that's all.

MAN THREE

But you told us we weren't to be hunted.

Man Two and Woman Three enter.

MAN

I know, I know. Uh—maybe we've been doing things wrong. We have to follow the Council's ways. Have we? If we haven't, we're going to have to stop what we're doing today and go back to the old ways.

MAN TWO

What? We can't go back to the old times, because we're too large in numbers. We've made families live in one den until it can't hold any more. We're now growing so large, our towns have become dirty and overcrowded.

MAN

If we're going to build more, we have to be certain that the trees we take won't destroy someone's home. We have to honor the markings of other nations. It's one of the Council's ways.

WOMAN TWO

I have to let my children freeze in the snow and rain so some bird or squirrel or raccoon is safe? No! I have to take trees now to build onto the home I have.

MAN

What—what about food? We all have enough to make it through this season. So if anyone hunts, we can share . . .

WOMAN TWO

Maybe you have enough to eat, but I don't.

MAN THREE

We are just as large as they are in numbers. They should change their ways and listen to us. We could add some new ways so we could live together.

MAN

If it weren't for them, we wouldn't have survived or grown to what we are today.

MAN THREE

But we have survived, and we should have a say in what we do. We are people, human beings. We are the new beings who will rule this world. We have ways—"laws."

MAN

Laws? What are those?

MAN THREE

Laws are the rules of how the nation of Man will live and how the nations of the Council will live under Man.

MAN

We can't change the ways overnight. The ways have been here for ages. Longer then any of us have.

MAN THREE

The laws will give us harmony with the animals. The first law is, Man can kill for food, to protect, to secure his property, and when he feels the urge. Second, all animals are beneath Man and should obey and serve Man. Third, Man has the right to use the trees, waters, air, and ground to enrich life for himself and his family. And finally, Man has the right to enter any territory or home that belongs to an animal and make it his property.

Some of the people respond with cheers.

WOMAN ONE

No, no. These laws don't sound fair to me. What about the children and women?

MAN THREE

They will be included in the laws as well, under Man.

WOMAN ONE

I can't live like that. No one should live like that.

MAN THREE

You will. You all will. If there are those of you who believe in what I say, go back to your homes and get your knives and spears.

MAN TWO

Let's do it.

WOMAN

Stop. It isn't right. We are a nation of the Council. We have to keep the Council's ways.

WOMAN ONE

Yes. We've come so far from where we used to be . . .

MAN THREE

Quiet! We will not be attacked by these animals!

MAN

Listen to me. Wait. Let me—let me try to call for a Council, and all of you can come with me. We'll go to the Council and ask them not to hunt us, or just to give us some more time. And maybe have the laws included with the ways.

Man Three stalks Woman.

WOMAN

Yes. Man is trying to do the best for all of us. We should (*Man Three grabs her*) . . . Let me go!

MAN

This is going too far.

Man Three signals Man One and Man Two to hold Man back by spearpoint.

MAN THREE

Stay back, Man. You stay away from the Council. If you go there, you'll never see Woman again. Take her and put her behind the wall with us. You others, take Man and put him outside the wall. Hurry! Do as I say!

MAN

But the Council will help us. I have to go.

WOMAN

Run, Man! Don't worry about me.

MAN THREE

Stop. Because if you do, you'll pay for it. Everyone at the Council will pay for their betrayal of us. (*Man is held at bay by Man Two and Man One. He knocks their spears away and exits.*) You fools! Don't stand there. Follow him and find out where he goes. We'll find those beasts and teach them to obey.

Man One runs after Man. Blackout.

SCENE SEVEN

Lizard is flying on the back of Condor. Condor makes a turn in the sky, and Lizard doesn't follow. He floats for a moment and then falls.

LIZARD

Oh, oh . . . OW!

Tiger, Panda Bear and Walrus enter.

TIGER

Lizard? Are you all right?

LIZARD

Silliness.

TIGER

Where are Man and Ice Traveler?

LIZARD

Just plain silliness.

PANDA BEAR

At least you came in a thud and not a splat.

TIGER

Man? Ice Traveler? This is useless. Where are those two?

Wolf enters.

WOLF

A pack of men surrounds the Council.

WALRUS

How dare they?

Council members are upset. Man enters, riding on the back of Ice Traveler. Man calls to Council members.

MAN

Members of the Council, hear me.

ICE TRAVELER

We have very little time. Everyone listen to him.

MAN

We must have new ways.

TIGER

What? What are they saying?

PANDA BEAR

Slow down, Man. Catch your breath. We can't understand you.

Man has landed and crosses to the center.

MAN

My people—my people will hurt us if we don't obey their laws.

LIZARD

Now it's "we." When did you decide to become one of us?

MAN

They want their laws included in the ways. We have to do it, if we all want to live in peace.

WOLF

Do you really talk for your nation? Is it going to be safe here?

Reaction from the Council members.

MAN

All you have to do is include some of their laws in the ways of the Council. It will be a peace offering to my nation.

LIZARD

What? Wait. What are laws, Man?

MAN

One law says we aren't going to be your equals.

TIGER

I like that. This could be interesting. What else?

MAN

We aren't going to be below you.

PANDA BEAR

Then what are you going to be?

MAN

Above you.

Council members are angered.

They believe they are the new beings, beings of Man. They will one day rule over you and your nations.

TIGER

We can't accept this.

ICE TRAVELER

But it could bring peace to all of us. There is a danger rising, and we must stop it.

PANDA BEAR

This is not natural. One being more important than another? The ways have always kept the nations together as one.

MAN

Wait, wait—that's just one of their laws. Listen, if you adapt the laws into the Council's ways, we'll have peace and the Council will survive.

TIGER

Don't worry about the Council, Man. We already have peace and harmony. (*Signals for the Council meeting to begin, and the members assume their positions in the circle.*) Now, everyone knows that no one is to be hunted going to or leaving a Council, but there are some men of your nation who are doing this.

MAN

I'll tell them to go home. Just please allow them to have some of their laws.

LIZARD

Man. The Council's way is "Kill only for food or to protect," not "Kill because you can't have what you want."

WOLF

Or "Kill because someone doesn't agree with you."

LIZARD

If we accept your laws, will this make your people stop hunting us?

MAN

I don't know if they will.

WALRUS

Then I say no to your laws. Members of the Council, do you agree?

Council members begin to vote.

MAN

Help me, Ice Traveler.

ICE TRAVELER

Listen to me.

Vote is completed.

TIGER

It has been decided, Ice Traveler.

Walrus exits.

ICE TRAVELER

All of Man's laws can't be bad. They are something we should consider. These are new times for all of us. There have been so many changes, and the world is unbalanced. If we could help Man, these laws could be a way to restore the harmony we've had.

TIGER

The Council has done what it could to help Man and his nation.It is enough. (*There are a flash of red cloth and muffled sounds.*) Be still.

WOLF

What's wrong?

Panda Bear sniffs the air.

PANDA BEAR

F-f-fire!

WOLF

They are breaking the circle of life.

The Council members scatter except for Tiger, Ice Traveler, and Man.

MAN THREE

(*From offstage.*) Get those beasts! Hurry! Don't let any of them escape. Kill them if you have to.

MAN

No! You can't do this! Not here.

Tiger stalks Man.

TIGER

You and your nations have gone too far.

ICE TRAVELER

Run, Tiger. Don't hurt him. It's not his fault.

MAN

Please, Tiger. Don't hurt me.

TIGER

How can a pitiful being like you force me to change into something I don't want to be.

Lunges at Man and misses.

I will never be the same because of you, but this time, you'll answer for it.

She tries to lunge again but misses. Man and Ice Traveler exit. She exits. A red banner appears onstage and sweeps the area. The muffled sounds now become shouts of anger from the nation of Man. Then the voices become silent. Wolf, Panda Bear, and Sea Turtle enter. The sound of grass being whacked at is heard. The three see each other and sense it is wrong. They turn to exit, but Man Three and some other humans enter.

MAN THREE

Get them! Don't be afraid! They are only animals. Tie them. Make sure you tie their binds tight. Hurry. Don't worry about the turtle. Work on the other two. (*The men tie Panda Bear and Wolf. They place a muzzle on Wolf. Sea Turtle has been placed on her back with a rock on her chest. The men exit.*) We'll come back for them later.

WOLF

What do you think they will do to us?

SEA TURTLE

Oh—I don't want to think about it. I bet it will be bad.

WOLF

How do we get out?

SEA TURTLE

We are never going to get out.

PANDA BEAR

What is she. . . . What are you doing, Wolf?

Wolf is trying to howl as Sea Turtle cries.

WOLF

Crying. And if I didn't have this thing on my mouth I could cry louder.

PANDA BEAR

Don't give up. Come on, you two. Please don't give up. We can get out of here. There is a possibility. Possibility leads to hope, hope leads to a solution. (*He struggles with the leash and ropes and breaks free, then he gets to his feet and stretches.*) Ahh, that feels good. (*He pushes the rock off of Sea Turtle and turns her over, then crosses over to Wolf and starts to chew on her muzzle.*)

WOLF

Ow! Watch where you're biting!

PANDA BEAR

Excuse me, but it blends so well with your color.

They get the muzzle off and she is able to free herself. They get together in a small group.

WOLF

Now what do we do?

PANDA BEAR

We'll sneak out together. Once we get some distance between us and the men, we'll try to find Ice Traveler. We will have Ice Traveler talk with Man. Maybe Man can talk with his people, hold a Council just for his nation. Hopefully we can have peace and restore the harmony we had.

WOLF

Then we must move quickly.

They start to leave Sea Turtle.

SEA TURTLE

Wait, wait. What about me? I can't keep up . . .

Panda Bear and Wolf without hesitation return to help Sea Turtle. They lift Sea Turtle onto Panda Bear's back.

PANDA BEAR

Now, everyone—please be quiet.

They sneak off. Blackout.

SCENE EIGHT

Man is trying to fish with no success. Mako enters and makes a noise.

MAN

Ice Traveler? Is that you? Ice Traveler?

No response. Mako makes a noise again.

Ice Traveler? I've . . .

Mako swims around Man, cutting off any escape.

MAKO

Hellos, and smiles pretties for us. It is we, my little crunchy, munch. Smackities, smackities.

Man raises his harpoon.

MAN

Get away from me!

MAKO

No, no—we no wants to get away from you. We wants to get closer to you, even better, so close, you be insides we forever. Yes, my little crunchies, munchies.

MAN

Get away! Leave me alone!

Stabs at Mako with the harpoon and then throws it at Mako and misses.

MAKO

Miss. He misses us, he really does. Now. We plays a game with it. Firsties, we goes out a little further. We needs more room to play. Yes, little man. Munchy, crunchies is ours. Yes it is. Now go.

Chases Man out to sea.

MAN

Help! Get away from me, Mako.

MAKO

Oh, what's wrong? We not wants to frightens, we wants crunchy munchies. Now swim faster, hurries, we wants to play.

Goes underwater and nudges Man.

MAN

Wait. Let's play a game.

MAKO

Smackity, smackities. We arezies. We's playing, I am hungry, and you is crunchy, munchies.

MAN

No. Help me! Help!

ICE TRAVELER

(*From offstage.*) Leave him alone!

MAKO

No, no—it is her again.

Ice Traveler enters.

ICE TRAVELER

I've told you to keep away from him.

MAKO

We wills, we wills, for now. Don't bumps and bites us. Pretties and pleases.

Begins to exit and stops.

We plays next time. You brings friends and we brings friends, we haves feeding frenzies!

Mako exits.

ICE TRAVELER

Get on my back, Man. There is something we have to do, and we don't have much time.

MAN

What are you talking about, Ice Traveler?

ICE TRAVELER

We are the only hope for the nations if there is going to be peace and harmony in this world. We can show the beings that there is a possibility of living together as one.

MAN

Those days are gone. I'm a Man and you're an animal. We'll never be equal again.

ICE TRAVELER

Do you really believe that, Man?

MAN

I—I don't know, Ice Traveler.

ICE TRAVELER

The world needs all the nations to live together in peace. We did it before. It's a knowledge that will never die but is sometimes forgotten. We have to make the people remember. Even if we have to bump and bite everyone. Look. We are closer to the shore. See. There are people. They'll see us together, as one.

MAN

Ice Traveler, just you and I won't be enough to make them see that they're wrong.

They are near shore, and Man jumps off Ice Traveler.

I'll go to the shore from here, Ice Traveler. Alone.

Man begins to swim.

ICE TRAVELER

No, Man. Don't give up. What do I have to do to make all of you realize there is hope?

Begins to swim to shore.

I am Ice Traveler of the Orca Nation. We can live together as one in the circle of life. The people of my nation will try to get on land and find those who are willing to work together as one. Live as one. Hear me, I am Ice Traveler . . .

She beaches herself. Man follows her.

MAN

Get back into the water, Ice Traveler. Please.

Tries to move her.

Help me, Ice Traveler. I can't do this by myself. Please. Someone, anyone, we can't do this by ourselves. We need help from anyone who will give it. Please. I am Man, one of the nation of Man. We need your help.

Blackout.

EPILOGUE

Present day. Joey, Michelle, and the beached Whales.

WHALE ONE

This is history,

WHALES TWO AND THREE

Your history,

WHALES TOGETHER

Our history.

WHALE ONE

Can, can you,

WHALES TOGETHER

Help us?

MICHELLE

Yes. Um,

She goes to the water, cups her hands, and brings water to the whale.

Is it all right if I put water on you?

WHALE

Thank you. It feels good, little one.

JOEY

Are you hurt really bad?

WHALE TWO

Wait. Can—can you tell us if things are continuing as they have been? We are looking for someone who will listen and help.

MICHELLE

Help? Oh our daddy is getting someone to help you now. Why—why are you here?

WHALE ONE

We are looking for someone who will sit and hold a council with us. Those who will listen and help. There are others from other nations in this world who are having a hard time, and they don't know how to ask for help.

MICHELLE

We'll do it. We'll hold council with you. We can help you. I am Michelle.

JOEY

I am Joey.

CHILDREN TOGETHER

We are from the nation of Man.

Father and another man enter. Michelle and Joey cross to them and bring them near the whales. Blackout.

Sneaky

Characters

FRANK ROSE: In his mid-thirties, the eldest son

ELDON ROSE: In his early thirties, the middle brother of the family

KERMIT ROSE: In his early thirties, the baby of the family

JACK KENCE: a white male in his early forties, the second-generation owner of a funeral home

SCENE ONE

PLACE: In the yard outside the house.

TIME: Evening.

The wind is softly blowing. Frank and Eldon are by a fire that is slowly burning out. There are a few small boxes around the brothers.

FRANK

What do you think?

ELDON

I don't know.

Pause.

Yeah. I guess so.

FRANK

We did round everything up?

ELDON

Yeah . . . yeah. I did.

Pause.

What about the old blue steamer trunk?

FRANK

I found it in the root cellar.

ELDON

Too bad. Hey, what about those boxes of sewing patterns? Them too?

FRANK

Yeah. I got them, too.

ELDON

The pictures?

FRANK

Not all of them.

ELDON

Good.

FRANK

I kept some of them. Here, take a look.

Frank removes a small cigar box from a bigger box and hands it to Eldon. Eldon eagerly goes through it.

She doesn't want anyone to have these. Burn them when you're done.

ELDON

The Smithsonians would want these . . . and this one, and that one—damn! You think we did right?

FRANK

Yeah, just like when the old man passed away. Did the same thing, but at a different spot.

Frank takes a bible from a box, and Eldon spots it.

I guess we could . . .

ELDON

Don't throw the Bible on the fire, Frank! Jesus.

Eldon takes the bible.

Hey—you remember? Colleen Hammer came driving up and tried to get the old man's rifle—the octagon .22?

FRANK

Yeah. The way she came driving up with all those wooden apple boxes in the back of her old white Ford. Her small, squinty eyes looking around the place. And that greasy apron she wears, black spots on her dress.

Frank laughs.

We used to tease you about her. We told you she was your bride, picked out for you.

ELDON

Quit teasing me like that. No way. Not that bad. Oh yeah, oh yeah. She said her "cuzin" let her have the rifle. And all the time it was burning with the rest of Dad's stuff. I thought she was going to scream when you told her if she wanted it, to go and get it. The fire had melted the barrel into a **U** shape.

Pause.

Where is Colleen now, I wonder? I thought she would show up by now.

FRANK

Probably mad about something.

ELDON

Mad? What for? Because of the . . .

FRANK

You didn't marry her.

ELDON

Damn you, Frank. You're always . . .

FRANK

I'm just kidding you, Eldon. It's too early yet. The news hasn't gotten around. When the word does, she'll be stopping by. She'll come in that old Ford. Probably with a bunch of cardboard boxes in her trunk and plenty of her grandchildren to help her with her haul.

Kermit enters. He is singing and carries a small paper sack. He sets the sack near the porch, takes a bottle from the sack and drinks, then he sets the bottle down and goes to the fire.

FRANK

It'll be just a matter of time. She'll come waddling into the yard like a fat duck to water. I don't like . . . hey!

Pause.

Kermit? Why don't you go into the house and stretch out?

KERMIT

Ma?

ELDON

Oh Christ . . . yeah! Kermit, you look tired.

Turns his back.

KERMIT

Momma? Oh . . . momma . . .

Stands at the fire.

FRANK

Come on, Kermit. You need the rest.

Grabs Kermit's arm.

Let's go.

He starts to lead Kermit, but Kermit breaks free and staggers.

KERMIT

No . . . no! I can do it by myself.

ELDON

Hey, ringy! He's only trying to help you.

KERMIT

I can do it . . . I can do it! Fuck!

He mumbles, staggers to the porch, and sits, then takes out the bottle and drinks. Frank watches as Eldon lifts some of the pictures from the box and sticks them inside his shirt.

ELDON

How is he? Is he going to get real ringy on us? (*Softly.*) Frank? Frank?

FRANK

Speak up! He'll be all right.

ELDON

Are you sure?

KERMIT

Yeah! Don't lose any sleep, El. I'm not going to die. I can hear you, even though I don't want to . . . goddamn it! Paw-uk-nah-uk!

ELDON

Was he cussing at me again? Huh? I hate it when he cusses at me in Assiniboine.

FRANK

Don't worry, it's only drunk talk. Hey—but you'll have one hell of a hangover tomorrow.

No reply from the brothers.

Christ. I remember drinking with him four years ago. He met me on a Friday night at the Long Horn. Denise took the kids and her mother to bingo.

Kermit gets up and walks over to the brothers, trying to hide the bottle on his way over.

KERMIT

You bet, partner! What yah guys doing?

FRANK

I wasn't planning anything. Then I started drinking shots of whiskey and had a beer chaser. Glad people told me, otherwise I would've forgotten. Anyways, he came over and sat with me. And then it was park-the-car time. What was it you were drinking?

KERMIT

Top secret—mustn't tell. It was muscatel.

He laughs and offers Frank a drink on the side.

FRANK

No thanks. When the Long Horn closed we got two cases of beer and a jug of wine and went to a house party—it was a house, anyway. We finished the beer and wine and I passed out.

KERMIT

Wussed out.

FRANK

Saturday afternoon we woke up, hot and sweaty, in the truck. Bought another case of beer and went to—Clem's bar, I think? Yeah. And we drank until Clem's closed. We drove around and finished off the case. I quit drinking Sunday, and I think this guy went drinking until next Sunday.

KERMIT

Hey, hey, hey, Frank. You wussed out on me.

ELDON

See! This is what I mean.

KERMIT

Oh shit. You mad? Fuck! Good time, huh Frank?

Pats Frank on the back and looks at Eldon. He goes back to the porch.

My brother.

ELDON

Now that Mom is dead he'll . . .

FRANK

No, no . . . it's up to him. One way or another, he'll decide for himself like I did.

ELDON

Are we going to have a feast after the funeral?

FRANK

Yeah. Claire said she would do it. The kids will help. Aunty Babs, Joan, and Ava said they would help, too.

ELDON

When are we going to have the funeral?

FRANK

Wednesday.

ELDON

Why Wednesday? Hell, that's a four-day wait. Hell, that's two days after we're supposed to have the feast!

FRANK

I know.

ELDON

Kence just wants it on Wednesday cause he can make more money. Keeping her in storage like a piece of furniture.

FRANK

He's the only mortician in a hundred miles. Hell—I don't like him, but he's the only one nearby.

Pause.

Hey!

ELDON

What?

FRANK

Why don't we bury Mom ourselves?

ELDON

You mean, let Kence prepare the body and we dig the hole?

FRANK

I've been thinking. We don't need to put all those chemicals and preservatives in her body. Why preserve her dead body like she was a damn beet?

ELDON

I don't know, Frank . . .

FRANK

Well, I sure the hell do.

ELDON

Yeah, but Father Crane will be pissed if he doesn't get to pray over her.

FRANK

To hell with Crane. He was there when she died. He had a chance to sprinkle his water on her and pray over her.

ELDON

If you think about it that way . . .

FRANK

Remember when I used to work for Kence Senior? He told me the secret for funerals, El. You want to know what they are? One—you need a dead body. Two—a hole in the ground. Three—transportation to get the body to the hole in the ground. Four—start a bank account.

ELDON

No . . . uh-uh . . . no . . . no . . .

FRANK

Don't worry, I'll take care of you.

Pause.

We have a right to do this. Even Kermit.

ELDON

Not that drunk.

FRANK

We're all family.

ELDON

But what about Dad's relatives?

FRANK

We did right by Dad—they'll think we did the same with Mom. We have to stick together and ride this one out. The others—they'll figure it out.

ELDON

Frank . . . Frank . . .

Pause.

You're just . . . You're really serious about this?

FRANK

Damn right I am.

ELDON

I thought you were just joking.

FRANK

No. And I'm not doing it because I'm trying to get out of Kence's fee. We'll give him his money when we're finished. I want us to bury her. Not a stranger and with his strange ways.

ELDON

How will we do it?

FRANK

She's always talked about being buried in the traditional way, remember?

ELDON

Yeah? Where are we going to start shoveling?

FRANK

Nooo . . . Eldon, no—not their way, our traditional way. Not buried in the ground. Bury her with the wind, in a tree.

ELDON

What about her decaying smell, in the wind?

FRANK

If you're worried about the smell, we can burn the body after the funeral. Just like in the old days, no one will find it. We can find an old tree and place wood around it and set them on fire.

ELDON

Then, why don't we just have her cremated? I'll pay for part of the cost.

FRANK

You're not listening. It isn't the money that's important. Way back when, it was the responsibility of the family to bury their own.

ELDON

That was a long time ago. Two or three hundred years ago. It wasn't right, remember?

FRANK

For who, Eldon? Us? Eldon—this way, her grave won't be disturbed. They uncover a bunch of unmarked graves and take the bodies out and in a few more years, who knows? Some scientist will come along and discover Mom's body and take it off to some college or university. Her skull sitting on a little wood box under glass. Her bones sawed up, spine and all, like beef ribs. Then they'll put them under a microscope. Is that right? I sure the hell don't think so. And I'm not going to allow it to happen.

Pause.

Goddamn it, El.

ELDON

Well, do you really know how to bury her in the traditional way? I don't recall having heard of anybody doing it recently. I don't know of anyone who has done it or remembers seeing it. And if nobody knows how to do it, I don't want to mess with it.

FRANK

You don't, huh? I remember Grandma telling us how they used to do it. And I remember a little of what Grandpa told me.

ELDON

Yeah? But do you know enough about it so we can do it right?

FRANK

Grandma told me how to do it. And I know she told it to you and Kermit when she used to baby-sit us. If we try to do it right, and do—do it right, we'll tell our kids about it. And they'll tell their kids. We can keep it going just like Grandpa and Grandma did with us.

ELDON

But what about the law? Her will? And if we're not caught by the cops, we still have Kence to settle with. And I don't want to mess with that guy.

FRANK

I've seen the will.

ELDON

How did you see it?

FRANK

In her last couple of weeks, she called me to her house and asked me to be with her. That's when she made her will out. Kence was there, too.

ELDON

Why didn't Mom call me?

FRANK

I don't know. Mom probably didn't want to bother you.

ELDON

I would have come if somebody would have told me. They call me for everything else. Christ! What the hell was Kence doing there? I'm her own son.

FRANK

Anyway—in her will she was going to request to be buried near the place she grew up at. She wanted to be buried in the traditional way. And Kence told her it wasn't possible. He knew where she wanted to be buried at, but he didn't know how to perform the ceremony. And he suggested she go with the American traditional funeral, everybody else does.

Pause.

ELDON

Well, why didn't you say something then, Frank? Huh?

FRANK

Not in front of Kence. He would've really put the blocks to us before we even had a chance.

ELDON

It just doesn't seem right. We could get caught.

FRANK

Who's going to know, huh?

ELDON

Someone will see us and tell. Maybe one of Mom's friends . . .

FRANK

They won't tell. I'll explain it to them. I'll put the will in the tribal newspaper if you want me to. Will and all. El, Mom didn't like the white man's funeral. She said all it had to do with is money, and nothing else. You can't even cry without the priest's permission.

Kermit slowly staggers to them.

If you decide no, we can't do it. You're the second to the oldest.

ELDON

If you can't do without me . . . I'm a member of the family now, huh? Okay, I'll go along with you, but we have to keep this to ourselves. I don't want this going through the moccasin telegraph.

FRANK

It'll go through the moccasin telegraph. By the time it gets around the rez, it'll be too late for Kence and the cops to do anything.

ELDON

It sounds slick and all. I . . .

KERMIT

What's up?

Tries to place his hand on Frank's shoulder.

FRANK

Kermit. We've decided to bury Mom ourselves. What do you think?

KERMIT

E-chaw-wok-nok! Hell, yes! Let's do-er!

He nearly walks into the fire, but is saved by Frank.

ELDON

Chh . . . Christ! He's not even in walking condition. Frank, if we get caught it'll be because of him. He's lost his mud. He hasn't cared about Mom. He's lived off of her. Now he wants to help us steal her from the morgue, because you've come up with this idea.

KERMIT

What? Steal Momma?

FRANK

Hold on now, Eldon. He has the right to be a part of this too. You wouldn't like to bury Mom by yourself?

KERMIT

Yeah, you tight-ass human.

ELDON

Shut up!

FRANK

I want us to do the burying, because that's the way we've always done things. By ourselves—family. We didn't get to bury Dad, but now we've got a chance to bury Mom as a family.

KERMIT

What's this shit about stealing Momma?

FRANK

We're going to take Mom from the mortician and bury her ourselves. Are you in?

KERMIT

Shit—yeah!

He falls and Frank tries to catch him.

ELDON

Oh, goddamn it!

FRANK

Don't be afraid of Jack Kence. I'll handle him.

ELDON

Like you did at Mom's will? I'm not afraid of him. Who said I was?

KERMIT

Fuck you. You're afraid of him because he has money. I'm not. I'm like Frank.

ELDON

Shut up, you drunk.

He goes to Kermit and pushes him.

FRANK

Easy, Eldon. I know Kence has money and a lot of connections, but he also has our mother.

KERMIT

Yeah. Who we talking about again?

FRANK

We're going to get her back. When Mom died, no one asked me what I wanted. Kence just came in and took her without permission.

ELDON

Yes, but he has a right, Frank. He's a mortician. The county coroner. It's his job.

FRANK

Its our job, Eldon. And the thing is, we don't get paid for doing it.

KERMIT

That's right. We can't let the son of a bitch do our job for us.

ELDON

What if he calls the cops on us? Huh? Or even the FBI? We could be up shit creek without a paddle. And if we go to jail? Hell, the pen? What happens to my family?

KERMIT

They'll be better off.

ELDON

Shut up, Kermit! You don't have a wife and kids to worry about. I do. And you have kids, too, Frank. What happens to them? How are we going to support them from prison?

FRANK

We won't get caught, El. Your problem is you're always thinking like one of them. So what if Kence has connections with the cops? That's the risk we have to take.

ELDON

Okay.

KERMIT

You're damned right. I'm behind you one hundred percent.

He goes into a fast grass dance, does a few steps, and nearly falls over into the fire but is saved by Frank.

FRANK

We're not cooking fry bread. If you burn yourself up, you aren't going to be worth a shit to us.

ELDON

You're not as it is now.

KERMIT

Sure I am. I can keep watch for you two guys. No problem.

FRANK

Okay. Let's get started.

ELDON

What about the fire.

Eldon picks up some of the boxes and turns his back to the brothers.

FRANK

We'll shovel dirt on it.

Eldon walks off.

ELDON

One big chief and a damn drunken Indian.

FRANK

What?

KERMIT

Damn right.

Kermit attacks the fire, and Frank helps him toss dirt onto it. Blackout.

SCENE TWO

PLACE: Jack Kence's funeral home.

TIME: Late at night, same day.

Frank and Eldon hide behind and run to several objects before they reach the funeral home. They enter the funeral home, and Frank leads Eldon to the surgical room. Kermit slowly follows his brothers. Two slabs are in the middle of the room with a surgical tray at the side of each slab, and a large sink on one side of the wall. The other wall is lined with glass and wood cabinets, each cabinet containing surgical equipment. Bodies lie on each slab. The brothers are carrying flashlights.

ELDON

God, it smells funny in here. What is that smell, Frank?

FRANK

Death and all its causes.

Eldon's light shines on the bodies.

ELDON

Hey! There are two of them. How do we know which one of them is Mom?

FRANK

You do the one on the right and I'll do the left.

Kermit enters the room. He is humming the theme song from a popular spy series. The two brothers go to the bodies. Kermit goes to Eldon. Frank is the first in pulling back the sheet.

FRANK

I found her. I found Mom.

Eldon pulls back the sheet and looks at Frank. Frank shakes his head "no," then Eldon looks at the body.

ELDON

Ohhh . . . my god. . .

KERMIT

What's up, El? Can't handle it, eh?

Eldon shows Kermit the body, and they become sick.

Ohhhh. . .

FRANK

Hold on. Hang on to it.

Eldon gets sick. Frank grabs Eldon and Kermit, and takes them to the sink. Frank goes back to the slab and examines the body. He finds a foot tag.

Jesus. It's Uncle Joe Yellow Foote, and half his face is gone.

Kermit and Eldon take turns vomiting into the sink. Frank reads the foot tag.

Accident victim: Hit and run. Identification: Joseph Alvin Yellow Foote, Senior. Occupation: Vagrant.

ELDON

God—it made me sick. Let's get the body and go.

FRANK

You're right, Eldon. Kermit? Can you make it back to the pickup by yourself?

KERMIT

Who, who—who hit me?

He is on his hands and knees rocking back and forth. Slobber dangles from his mouth and touches the floor. He slumps to the floor.

Son of a bitch! Who hit me, goddamn it! Come on! I'll take you all on. . .

FRANK

Better help him out to the truck, El. He won't make it by himself.

ELDON

Frank! I can't! Are you going to carry Mom by yourself?

FRANK

No. But he needs help—now!

KERMIT

Float like a butterfly, sing like a bee-grasshopper.

ELDON

We'll get caught. I know it.

FRANK

El, listen to me. You help Kermit back to the truck and I'll clean up this mess. Then come back and help me.

Frank walks back to Kermit and helps him to his feet.

KERMIT

Bring them on—bring them all on. . .

ELDON

All right, all right. I'll do it.

KERMIT

Frank. . . Frank? Oh, there you are. We'll take them all on. . .

FRANK

Right, Kermit.

Eldon and Kermit begin to walk out the door.

KERMIT

Oh—Christ! Momma!

FRANK

Hurry up, El. Just do it and be sure to come back and help me.

KERMIT

Hey, you guys. Bathroom. Guys—bathroom!

Eldon finds a place to grab Kermit and leads him out the door. Frank starts a search for paper towels. He finds them and wets them in the sink, then he starts to wipe the floor where Kermit was and then the sink. He looks for a garbage can and finds one, but it is filled. He steps on the pedal of another can, and the lid opens. Frank crams the paper towels into the can, a disposal can for dead organ and tissue. Frank nearly vomits. He washes his hands and is faced again with the task of disposing of the paper towels. He wads them up and puts them in his shirt pocket, glances around the room and does a quick go-over of it, checks the floor and then the two slabs. He goes over to his mother and gently removes the blanket from her face.

FRANK

Ma, I don't. . . I don't know if I can live without you. You've always given me your support. Helped me out when I needed it. My whole family loves you. We're all going to miss you.

Eldon enters. He stops and watches.

You've worked hard all your life, Mom. And now you suffer no pain. Thank you for being our mother. It'll be really tough without you in this world. We'll try. And we'll always remember you. Damn. I don't know if I can carry this whole family, Mom. Please help me find a way to do it—or to let go.

Pause.

We should all be going and just let go.

ELDON

Frank? Frank?

FRANK

Goodbye, Uncle Joe. . . What is it?

ELDON

There's a security cop. Are you all right?

FRANK

Yeah.

ELDON

Well, there's a security cop. I thought he saw me and Kermit, so I headed down the alley.

FRANK

Where's Kermit?

ELDON

I put him in a garbage bin. We'll get him later.

FRANK

Damn.

ELDON

He'll be all right. He doesn't even know what's going on. When I put him in, he gave me his wallet. Let's get Mom.

They both go to the body and pick it up. A light shines under the door.

FRANK

Oh-oh! Someone's coming, El.

ELDON

You take her.

He drops his end of the body. Frank hangs onto his end.

FRANK

What the hell are you doing, El? Just pick her up, and we'll take her and put her back on the slab and hide.

They do, then hide, Frank behind a cabinet and Eldon alongside of Joe, covering himself with Joe's blanket. The door opens, and a ray of light sweeps the room. The light stops and the door closes.

El? El? I think it's okay. Let's go. Where are you?

ELDON

Oh. . . man.

He climbs out from under the sheet. Frank crosses to him.

FRANK

Don't feel bad. I would have done the same thing.

ELDON

I feel like one of those microwave sandwiches. Okay—I'm sorry I dropped Mom. I want to go now. I don't want to hang around here.

FRANK

You're not the only one. We'll have to wait a bit.

ELDON

Why? The guard is gone. Don't know why you'd need a guard at a funeral home anyway.

FRANK

Somebody might steal something.

ELDON

Oh, Christ.

FRANK

Really. There are a lot of expensive things around here. When I was working here, somebody stole some clothes.

ELDON

Clothes?

FRANK

Yeah. Kence has clothes that zip up in the back. It makes it easier for him to dress the body.

ELDON

Who stole them?

FRANK

Remember that one year all the winos around town looked real sharp?

ELDON

Jesus. How could they? Let's go.

Frank goes to the door and looks out. Eldon sniffs himself.

FRANK

It looks okay, but let's wait for a bit more. He was probably making his rounds.

Crosses to Eldon.

ELDON

Do I stink?

FRANK

Sometimes—that's why I always stand left of you. Nah, but not now. You're okay.

ELDON

Okay, but I want to get cleaned up before we have the funeral and get a star quilt. We're not going to bury Mom in this.

FRANK

Crosses to the door and checks.

All right.

Crosses back to Eldon.

It's okay. Ready?

Picks up one end of the body and Eldon picks up the other.

ELDON

Frank? Are you scared?

FRANK

Yeah. Let's take Mom and make some tracks.

They carry the body out, stopping on the way to pick up Kermit. They carry Kermit and the mother in the blanket. Blackout.

SCENE THREE

PLACE: Five miles from town, near the river and a clearing of a meadow.

TIME: Early in the morning, next day.

There is a human mound—Kermit and the body. Kermit stirs and rolls off the body, rolls near a small fire, and shakes a little from the morning cold. Then he reaches out to wrap a blanket around himself. The blanket isn't there. He slowly wakes up. He rests himself on his elbows and tries to refocus his eyes. He sees his mother with her blanket.

KERMIT

Damn, it's chilly.

Pause.

Did you go to the softball tournament, too? I didn't see you. You probably seen me.

No reply.

I sure am cold . . . and lonesome.

Leans towards her.

You know, hey? You know, you have a blanket. And I don't have any. Brr. . . . And I suppose you're cold, too.

He touches her.

Damn . . . damn! You're really cold . . . freezing.

Touches himself.

Hey! Hey there, partner. I tell you what. You share your blanket with me. I'll be good.

No reply.

Don't worry. Don't worry, honey. I won't hurt you even if you don't want to share your blanket.

No reply.

Don't be stuck up. I'll even let you sleep near the fire. Be, be—be sure you don't burn yourself from the sparks.

No reply. Kermit begins to pull at the blanket.

Don't be a tight ass. Come on baby. Share with me.

Eldon and Frank enter.

Baby . . . darlin'. Baby cakes?

ELDON

After I showered up—I guess the cops called while I was showering, and my wife told them I was sleeping, and . . .

KERMIT

Oh, baby. Ohhh . . . baby, baby, sweet baby cakes . . .

He caresses his mother's shoulder.

ELDON

What the hell is he doing? I thought he was passed out.

FRANK

How the hell do I know.

KERMIT

Yeah. Ohhh . . . baby . . .

He uses his other hand to caress his mother.

ELDON

Oh shit!

Runs over and kicks Kermit away.

KERMIT

Ow! Fuck!

ELDON

Frank, did you see what he was doing?

FRANK

Yeah. Kinda hard to miss it, El.

KERMIT

I wasn't doing anything wrong. Fuck. I was doing it with love.

ELDON

I thought you said if we left him alone, passed out, he wouldn't do anything.

FRANK

I was wrong.

ELDON

Do something then, Frank!

FRANK

What? What do you want me to do, Eldon?

KERMIT

It's just a girl. Christ. Eldon fucking freaks out on everything. Shit!

ELDON

A girl? You don't know, do you? Frank—he doesn't even know.

FRANK

He's been drinking, Eldon. He just must be coming out of it.

ELDON

All right, Frank. A girl, huh? Come here.

Grabs Kermit and pulls him near their mother's face.

It's Mom, Kermit. It's your mother.

Kermit looks at the face.

FRANK

Kermit?

KERMIT

Oh, god damn . . .

He crawls away from the body and scratches the ground.

Damn . . . damn . . . it . . .

ELDON

I had to, Frank. And you, Frank—you are going to have to stop taking care of him. You bought him that wine tonight. He has to live down whatever he does.

KERMIT

Keep away from me.

FRANK

Come on, you guys. Knock it off.

KERMIT

Why the hell did you guys have to do that, huh?

ELDON

Because you are a drunk. You can't be blaming what you do on being drunk all the time, Kermit. I don't want my little brother to be a drunk.

KERMIT

Yeah? Well, you're an apple, red on the outside. Hell! You're white all over, in and out. You're a white man. We should cut you out.

ELDON

What? No, I'm your brother.

FRANK

Don't say any more, you two.

KERMIT

You know what Mom used to say, Eldon? Huh? She used to say how she raised two Indin sons and one businessman.

ELDON

That's a lie.

KERMIT

Don't believe me? Ask Frank. She said one loves celebrations, one loves hunting and building things, and the other one loves money.

ELDON

She didn't mean it that way, Kermit. That's not true.

KERMIT

You're a white man, Eldon. I hate to see one of my older brothers turn into a white man. You dress like Jack Kence—you even smell like him.

ELDON

Stop it, Kermit.

KERMIT

Mr. Chamber of Commerce. Only Indin there. Yeah. And you're such a big wheel. You and your stink smoke shack. Indins around here are laughing at you behind your back.

ELDON

I don't give a shit about that.

KERMIT

That's probably why you wanted all of Mom's things. So you could sell them at your smoke shack.

ELDON

No, it was for my girls. They deserve . . .

KERMIT

Mr. Businessman. Last Thanksgiving, when you put that big cardboard cut of a turkey around your smoke shack, the stink little trailer. No one else, but you. Ohhh . . . shit! All the places I've been. All the Indin people I know. You're the only one who celebrates Thanksgiving, the coming of the white man. But then again, it's like welcoming your brothers, enit? You break your ass recognizing them, but you sure as shit can't recognize me when you see me on the streets, can you?

ELDON

I've always come to help.

FRANK

Don't be talking about these things now, Kermit.

KERMIT

Why not? Now's a good time as any. He'll leave and forget all about us. Ignore us when he sees us, because we're Indins and he's not.

ELDON

I only ignored you one time, Kermit! One time! And that's because you were sitting on the steps of the Sherman Hotel. You've probably forgotten that . . . I bet you don't even remember. You had puked all over yourself and didn't know it. Peed your pants, your hair was greasy and matted, and you didn't even know it. You were bumming people who were coming and going into the hotel. You were mumbling away. "Help me, help me." The cops wanted to take you in. They stopped at the smoke shack and told me, but I talked with them, promised them I would come and get you.

Pause.

And when I pulled up and parked my car, you were mumbling away, "Eldon, Eldon." I walked over to you, and you didn't even hear me when I called your name. You didn't even recognize my voice. You didn't even recognize me, period! You just kept on mumbling. I felt so bad for you. I picked you up and took you to my house and cleaned you up. And then, I . . . I cried. Ever since that time I told myself—I promised myself—if I ever saw you drunk like that again, I wouldn't recognize you. It would be easier for me if you were some other wino, but you're my brother.

Pause.

It is true, Kermit. I didn't recognize you. And there were times I didn't want to recognize Frank and Dad. All three of you were drunk. I'm a member of the family now, huh? You know what—what hurts me the most? You all three treated me like another drunk, not like a brother. Just because I didn't drink with you guys didn't mean I was too good for you guys. It just meant I was sober.

Pause.

The next time, Kermit . . . I will disown you.

KERMIT

See, see! Too fucking good!

FRANK

I would've done the same thing, Kermit.

KERMIT

No you wouldn't—no, Frank. You're my brother. Not like this guy.

ELDON

Damn you.

Charges Kermit.

FRANK

Don't, Eldon.

KERMIT

You want to fight, huh? I'll kick your fucking ass. Come on. You and the big son of a bitch, Frank. Both of you, come on!

FRANK

Knock it off, Kermit!

KERMIT

You're not so fucking good as you act, Frank.

FRANK

Shut up, Kermit!

KERMIT

But first I'm going to knock the shit out of this bastard. Yeah. You're both alike.

FRANK

You'd better settle down.

KERMIT

I don't have to. Damn it! Come on and fight!

He slaps Eldon. Eldon doesn't do anything. Kermit tries to dance around like a boxer. He tries to slap Eldon again, but Eldon grabs his arm and pulls Kermit to him and holds him. Kermit tries to break free.

Damn you! You fucking ass! Let me go! I can take care of . . . of myself.

Kermit stops struggling. Eldon loosens his hold. There is the sound of a car. Frank crosses to his brothers and touches them. The sound of the car becomes louder.

ELDON

What?

FRANK

Listen. I think it's a car.

ELDON

Maybe it's just a farmer.

FRANK

Too early. Did you close the gate?

ELDON

I think so.

FRANK

You'd better go check and see.

Eldon begins to exit.

Wait. We don't have time.

ELDON

What do we do?

FRANK

We have to hide Mom.

ELDON

Let's cover her up.

They cover her with the blanket.

FRANK

It won't work.

ELDON

What if one of us lies down and pretends we're sleeping . . .

They look at Kermit.

KERMIT

Oh, no, no!

FRANK

Come on, Kermit. You have to. Just this one time.

ELDON

If you do it, we don't have to come up with a good excuse . . .

KERMIT

No—ah, shit . . .

He starts to get to his knees. Eldon removes the blanket from their mother's body. Kermit lies on top of their mother and they cover them. Jack Kence enters.

FRANK

Be quiet, Kermit.

JACK

Good morning.

FRANK

Hello, Jack.

ELDON

Uh . . . hi, Jack.

JACK

Goddamn, it's chilly this morning. What're you boys doing out here so early?

ELDON

We—we're gathering a few things for the feast. You know, tea, meat, cheese . . .

JACK

Well, you guys shouldn't be spotlighting. It's illegal. Hard to do without any rifles.

ELDON

Jack . . . that's because we're not allowed to use rifles, traditionally. We use our cars.

JACK

Uh-huh.

FRANK

Calm down, Eldon. What're you doing here Jack?

JACK

I have one hell of a mess on my hands, Frank. You see, I got a phone call from my security man. It's kind of embarrassing. He said Elva Rose's body is missing.

ELDON

No!

JACK

Yes—said he saw your pickup outside of my place last night. Well, I kinda figured you might know where your mom's body is at.

ELDON

By golly, we don't know what the hell you're talking about, Jack.

JACK

Oh. I see. What's this over here?

ELDON

It's our baby brother. He's asleep.

JACK

Well, what's he laying on?

ELDON

Traditionally—straw.

Crosses to the body.

JACK

Let's take a look.

ELDON

Oh shit. Oh shit.

Eldon begins to take off but is stopped by Frank.

JACK

Kermit, come on kid. Get up.

Eldon crosses over to Jack and stops him from touching the blanket.

ELDON

I said, it's our baby brother Jack.

JACK

But this blanket is familiar.

Pulls on the blanket and then Kermit.

Get up, kid.

Rolls Kermit off the body.

Oh, Christ. Have you guys lost your marbles?

Jack examines the body.

Didn't really damage anything.

ELDON

Sorry, Jack . . .

JACK

Sorry, shit! Eldon. Help me take this back to my car.

FRANK

Take your hands off our mother, Jack.

JACK

Look, this is getting really sick. Now help me take your mother back to my place, and we'll forget all about this. Eldon?

ELDON

I can't.

JACK

Why not?

KERMIT

Why should he? You're just a white man.

JACK

Look, I know this is a difficult time, but I have a job to do. Now help me out and we can all go home and forget this happened. I'm not in a great mood, guys. I don't want to be out here all damn morning long. Let's go.

No response.

Frank, be reasonable. All right. Eldon, give me hand here? I'm taking this body back with me.

No response.

You fellas don't seem to understand this. We seem to have a hell of time communicating like normal people. She belongs to me—mine—and I still have a lot of work to do. I have to do some more preparations, dress her up, and I have a backup at the home and the sooner I can get this one done, I can move on. Now come on, El.

ELDON

I can't, Jack. My brothers and I have decided she's going to stay with us.

JACK

What?

FRANK

That's right, Jack. Our mother is staying with us.

JACK

All the times you worked with my father, Frank. I thought you were more reasonable than this.

FRANK

I am, Jack.

JACK

Not as far as I can see.

KERMIT

Then you must be blind and white.

JACK

Be quiet, kid. You guys can get into a lot of trouble for this. I'm not joking. I'd hate to see it happen.

FRANK

That's the chance we're willing to take.

JACK

I came here without notifying the police where I am. The cops, both tribal and white, are patrolling all around town and the surrounding area looking for your mother.

KERMIT

Did you tell them what she was wearing, hey?

JACK

Kermit, I've always heard you were a little drunken smart ass, but I didn't think it was this bad. Goddamn. If you guys don't give me some damn good reasons in the next few minutes, I'll have to go back to my car and call the cops out here. You can save us all a lot of trouble if you can give me a hand and take your mother's body back to my car, and I'll take it back with me.

KERMIT

Do it yourself. We don't work for you.

JACK

You know, Eldon, I remember a young man coming up, working very hard to succeed in business. Then making it. Becoming a member—the first Indian, mind you—to make the chamber of commerce. Now, to lose it all on one bad move . . . I know you must have had one hell of a battle with the bottle . . .

ELDON

Damn it, Jack! I never drank before. I don't drink now. I've never had no damn battle with any goddamn bottle. None of you know me.

FRANK

I think you'd better leave, Jack.

JACK

What the hell for? I don't have what's mine yet.

FRANK

We're going to bury Mom ourselves.

JACK

You are? Why?

FRANK

We know what type of funeral she wanted.

JACK

Then what kind is that Frank, huh? What kind?

FRANK

One that isn't bought and paid for. Doesn't come out from any showcase. She always wanted to be buried in the Indin way.

JACK

What do you think I would do? Put her in a pine box and leave her on the side of a hill, unburied?

FRANK

They don't do that any more—or do they?

JACK

You and your brothers are going to perform the funeral? You're the priest, he's the undertaker, and Kermit is the gravedigger?

FRANK

And if you notice, they're all family.

JACK

We have laws, health codes—state and federal. It isn't that simple.

FRANK

It was at one time. Just like dying was. Only you didn't have to pay anybody back then. And you had the time to say good-bye to the one you love. You didn't have to rush because the priest had an appointment, like a potluck. And our way means we don't have to worry about the price of a hearse or coffin, just the loss of the one we love.

JACK

You don't want your mom buried like the way white people do? And I'm so evil for that? You have to do better than that, Frank. A whole lot better. I've buried a lot of white people and your people in my days. They all have one thing in common—after a certain amount of time, they rot and they're forgotten.

FRANK

And I'm not going to let that happen.

JACK

But not with this body.

FRANK

You want a body, Jack? First, here. Here's some money.

Takes some bills out of his pocket and gives them to Jack.

This should take care of all the costs. And you want a body? Here. Take this one.

Pushes Eldon to Jack.

Or this one. Take this guy.

Pushes Kermit.

KERMIT

Behave, Frank. Wok-ne-kit-due.

JACK

Oh, Christ.

FRANK

You want a body? Take one of these guys, or hell—take me. You're going to get one of us sooner or later.

JACK

All right, damn it. You had your fun. You tell me one thing. What is the mandate of heaven you have that the rest of us don't? You seem to have taken all the weight and secrets of the world on your shoulders.

He walks up to Frank and puts the bills into Frank's pocket.

Go ahead.

FRANK

It's easy. When I say it, I mean it.

JACK

I'm getting tired and it's getting chillier. I'm thinking really seriously about getting the cops out here.

FRANK

You do that! You go ahead. I don't care what you do to us after the funeral. Just don't try to stop us from having it. I'm willing to sacrifice whatever I have to, Jack. Having this woman as a mother was a great gift. And now we're returning her back to her god, her family, her relations. We have an old woman to bury now, Jack. You can stay and watch or get into your car and drive off. It's a threat or an offer. Seriously—hey, it is serious—as serious as burying our mother. Now we have a funeral to start, Jack.

JACK

Frank, you can have your little funeral. Don't even bother to pay me. Listen to me—this is my threat, warning, or whatever the hell you want to call it. Don't you or your brothers ever cross me again. This is the last time and the first time it happens. I don't know if I can completely forget this. You guys sure the hell better hope I do.

He begins to exit.

I provide a service for people. You remember that. A service—and what they pay me for that service doesn't mean a thing. I do the work people can't. Enjoy your services.

Exiting.

For Christ's sake.

ELDON

Good-bye, Jack.

Crosses to Frank.

Do you think he'll call the cops?

FRANK

Wait.

ELDON

We sure the hell showed him though, huh? We'd better hurry up and start the funeral. If he tells the police, we won't have a chance.

FRANK

Wait a minute, El.

Car engine starts.

I'm going to be right back.

ELDON

You're not running out on us, are you?

FRANK

I said, I'll be right back.

Frank exits.

ELDON

Pretty shaky ground, huh, Kermit? Kermit? Hey, Kermit. What's wrong with you?

KERMIT

You don't know what's wrong? Christ. It's what I did to Mom. I do all kinds of things, but I can never remember.

ELDON

Yeah. I know.

KERMIT

What's that?

Sound of truck leaving.

ELDON

That's Frank.

KERMIT

Well? You still mad at me?

ELDON

Do you really want to know? You know, Kermit, when you're sober, I don't mind having you around. When you're drunk, you can be a pain in the ass. You're the last person I want to have around me. Never knew anyone I wanted to hurt as much as you. Too much has happened.

KERMIT

What about Mom?

ELDON

What about her? I mean, she really worried about you. She always thought you might accidentally get run over, freeze to death, hit by a train. Something she just couldn't have helped. It happened to Uncle Joe.

KERMIT

He wasn't really our uncle.

ELDON

We claimed him.

KERMIT

Do you claim me? Tell me the truth?

ELDON

You're my brother through blood. I could disown you. I don't know any more.

KERMIT

Ach-noc-chew-luke.

ELDON

What the hell does that mean?

KERMIT

It's Klingon. You know? Your girls watch it. Live long and prosper.

ELDON

All this time, I thought . . . hey. Why don't you and I learn to speak Assiniboine? Instead of using this false language to speak with. We can find someone to help us.

KERMIT

Just you and me, huh? I don't know. What if I bring someone else with me?

ELDON

No. This is something we can do ourselves, or we don't do it.

Frank enters.

FRANK

Ready?

He carries a sack.

KERMIT

Where'd you go?

FRANK

I used my pickup to block the road. Now no one can get in. Where's your quilt, El?

ELDON

Got it.

FRANK

You and Kermit roll Mom up in it.

Eldon spreads the blanket out. Frank and Kermit roll her up in it like rolling a cigarette. Frank places more wood around the tree.

ELDON

Done.

FRANK

Now we'll put her in the tree. El, you take her shoulders—that end. Kermit, you take a stick and push back the branches when we put her in.

They place the body into the tree. Frank sets the sack on top of their mother. He takes a braid of sweet grass from the back of his pocket.

KERMIT

Hey, what is that?

FRANK

Some tobacco and pemmican.

KERMIT

Oh, munchies.

FRANK

When I light this, we pray.

KERMIT

I hate to interrupt you, brother. Is there any special prayer we should say?

FRANK

Yeah. Your own.

He lights the sweet grass. Makes circles around the brothers and himself.

KERMIT

Now what, hey?

FRANK

I don't know. This is all I can remember.

ELDON

We should pray again, huh? The Lord's Prayer can be for Mom, as well as for white people.

FRANK

Awkwardly makes the sign of the cross.

Our father, who are in heaven, hello it be they name. Thy kingdom come . . . thy kingdom come . . .

KERMIT

Does it have to be done.

FRANK

Does it have to done on earth as it is in heaven. Give us our day and our daily . . . our daily . . .

KERMIT

Daily fry bread.

FRANK

Daily fry bread. And forgive us our sins as we forgive those who have . . . those who have . . .

KERMIT

Those who have thrashed ass against us.

FRANK

Yeah. Those who have thrashed ass against us. Lead us not into temptation O lord, but deliver us from, from, from . . .

KERMIT

Lies.

FRANK

Lies. Thank you, Kermit.

Kermit farts.

FRANK/KERMIT

You're welcome.

ELDON

O heavenly father. These two men here are my brothers. We've come to bury our mother on this morning. She was a good woman. In all this world, you have given us a great gift: each other, and most importantly, this woman. We thank you.

KERMIT

Is this all?

FRANK

I guess it is. I've got some stuff to make some torches back at my truck. Let's go.

KERMIT

You guys go ahead. I want to think about some things.

FRANK

Sure. Come on, El.

Frank and Eldon exit.

KERMIT

Ob la di, ob la da, life goes on, la la la . . . Frank? Frank?

To the body.

You're probably wondering why I called you here . . .

He laughs, starts to walk away, and nearly trips.

Ma? Ma! Don't do this . . . please . . . I, I—I don't know what to do. I don't know. I thought I'd know what to do. Honest. I really did.

Pause.

Ma?

Softly to himself.

Mom, I . . .

He goes to where Frank was standing, picks up the burning braid of sweet grass, tries to breath in the smoke and then lets the braid drop.

Damn.

He stands and looks at the body.

Ma, I don't know what to say. I always thought I'd know what to do when this time came. I know you've always been here for me. And now you're not here. Or are you? You can't tell me what to do or say. I guess now I have to go on my own. I hope. Goddamn it, Mom! When you . . . left me . . . I could feel the tear. And no matter how much I drank, it kept ripping inside of me. And then it got cold. Cold all over inside of me. You know, huh? You know what I'm talking about? Like you with Dad? Forgive me, Mom. It's all I ask. Please. I want you to know. I was afraid I would drown you out with the booze, but I'm happy I didn't. I couldn't. I don't even know why I tried. We'll live long and prosper. Now what? What?

He starts to hum a song. Frank and Eldon enter carrying torches. Kermit turns and waves them to join him. Without skipping a beat they join him, hold arms, and sing. Blackout.